BASICS
FASHION MANAGEMENT

FASHION
BUYING
From Trend Forecasting to Shop Floor

David Shaw/Dimitri Koumbis

Fairchild Books
An imprint of Bloomsbury Publishing Plc

50 Bedford Square
London
WC1B 3DP
UK

1385 Broadway
New York
NY 10018
USA

www.bloomsbury.com

FAIRCHILD BOOKS, BLOOMSBURY and the Diana logo are trademarks of
Bloomsbury Publishing Plc

British Library Cataloguing-in-Publication Data
A catalogue record for this book is available from the British Library.

PB: 978-2-94041168-9
ePDF: 978-2-94044754-1

Bloomsbury Cataloging-in-Publication Data
Shaw, David; Koumbis, Dimitri.
Fashion Buying: From Trend Forecasting to Shop Floor / David Shaw,
Dimitri Koumbis p. cm.
Includes bibliographical references and index.
ISBN: 9782940411689 (pbk. :alk. paper)
eISBN: 9782940447541
1. Fashion merchandising. 2. Fashion merchandising—Management.
HD9940 .S538 2013

Design Pony Ltd.
www.ponybox.co.uk

Printed in India

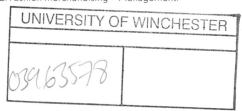

1980s Gordon of Philadelphi...
1980s Gord... $36.00 USD

1990s Pastel Geometric Prin...
1990s Paste... $32.00 USD

1990s Illustrated Leaf Patter...
1990s Illustr... $32.00 USD

1950s Enchantment Under t...
1950s Ench... $275.00 USD

1980s Electric Blue Snakesk...
1980s Electr... $66.00 USD

1970s Vintage Dolce & Gab...
1970s Vinta... $350.00 USD

Designer 1960s Eduardo for ...
Designer 19... $88.00 USD

1990s Cropped Classic Gue...
1990s Crop... $78.00 USD

1980s Womens Retro Chevr...
1980s Wom... $42.00 USD

Dazzling Magenta Silk Butto...
Dazzling Ma... $72.00 USD

1980s Colorful Tribal Print B...
1980s Color... $62.00 USD

1980s Bright Multicolored Sh...
1980s Brigh... $62.00 USD

1   SHOWCASING
    YOUR RANGE

Buyers aim to provide
consumers with various facets
of current fashion trends
combined: in this case, a trendy
vintage silhouette combined
with neon-bright shades.

TABLE OF CONTENTS

INTRODUCTION

The role of fashion buyer is commonly seen as one of the most glamorous jobs within the entire fashion industry. Often, people enter a career in fashion buying wrongly believing that the job is about buying clothes that they themselves would like to wear. Ultimately, however, fashion buyers need to know and understand about the latest trends, colors, styles, and brands that will appeal to their target consumer.

At every trading level, the fashion buyer's main task is to select best-selling lines that will appeal to their target customers and—more importantly—that will sell out quickly. Working closely with a designer and merchandise planner, it is the fashion buyer who ensures that the business is adequately stocked at the appropriate point of the season, with enough best-selling lines to meet the business's planned sales and profit.

Fashion Buying aims to explore what fashion buying actually entails in terms of the activities, processes, and people involved—all from the perspective of the fashion buyer. There are many different roles within fashion buying, ranging from buyers who create house brands for the lower-priced discounters and supermarkets, to those who work for high-end department stores selecting ranges from well-known prestige brands. Each level of buying requires a slightly different approach and each has its own nuances; but in general, most require the same processes, skills, and understanding—with only the customer being the changeable element.

Fashion Buying has been divided into the five main areas of buying activity: summary of the buying role, sources of fashion inspiration, key buying influences, merchandise and supplier management and planning, and internal and external relationship management. The book explores real-life fashion buying, that is, mainstream fashion buying—where most jobs and opportunities exist within the business.

1 SPRING/SUMMER 2010

Working Studio 54 chic, Riccardo Tischi's collection for Givenchy haute couture took inspiration from the early 1970s, evidenced in this giant pom-pom jacket complete with glitterball make-up. In the runway show, 22 ensembles were shown in just seven minutes.

"The goal I seek is to have people refine their style through my clothing without having them become victims of fashion."
Giorgio Armani

Introduction

Chapter 1

This chapter identifies the different types of fashion buying roles and also explains the significance and importance of the buyer in achieving business success. The intense and varied nature of the work is revealed, together with the importance of each individual buying and merchandising team. The skills, personality, and attitude needed for successful fashion buying are also touched upon which will prove useful to practitioners seeking to improve their own business opportunities.

Chapter 2

Buying is a highly creative skill, in part because fashion buyers must be continually responsive to an ever-changing fashion landscape; and to the ceaseless demands of today's savvy consumer. In this chapter, how buyers work with designers to continuously plan and buy new ranges, often seasons in advance of customers buying them, is demystified. The increasing use of in-house design teams and fashion forecasting services in order to get the product right is explored, and suggestions for the best sources of gaining fashion inspiration and guidance are provided.

Chapter 3

Throughout the developed world, home-produced fashion product is becoming increasingly rare, requiring fashion buyers to source product internationally. As consumer demands for quality and value increases, finding, managing, and developing effective and efficient foreign suppliers is a business fundamental.

In Chapter 3, we turn to look at the importance of successfully managing foreign suppliers, as well as at the issues at stake in producing the right range offer—in terms of lines, categories, and departments. Editing and controlling fashion ranges is a key buying activity—even though fashion buyers always want to buy far many more lines than they have money available to buy them! Increasingly, fashion buyers are involved in the process of showing their products to best advantage in shops and stores. This chapter reveals the dilemmas faced by today's buyers in final supplier and range selection.

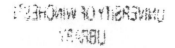

Chapter 4

In today's hyper-competitive fashion market, the need to get the right product to market at the right price, in the right place at the right time has never been more important. The fashion market is one of the most unforgiving. To this end, in this chapter we turn to examine how large fashion retailers undertake detailed levels of line and product planning to ensure that they present the best offer in the street.

We look at how merchandise planning increasingly constitutes a large part of the fashion buyer's activities and how the specialist merchandise planner (or 'merchandiser') works alongside the buyer enabling them to concentrate on the more creative aspects of the role.

Chapter 5

As retailers continue to grow, they formulate strategies that will help their firms to grow in a positive direction, taking into consideration all of the stakeholders involved in the process. In this final chapter, the concept of corporate social responsibility is introduced and we look at how the buyer's role can help foster CSR initiatives, both internally and externally. Chapter 5 also looks at various trends in buying, from promotional activities that generate demand for goods to technology that facilitates stronger communication between buyers and stores.

Within each chapter, you'll discover interviews with key fashion professionals, which put the contents of the chapter into context and perspective, offering you unique insights into the business of fashion buying and the challenges facing buyers today. Business case studies demonstrate the activities described and practical activities are suggested that enable you to work through the ideas explored in each chapter.

The actual fashion buying process represents only one stage along a long and very complex supply chain, which often involves hundreds of individuals. Fashion buying is also an intellectually demanding job, with so many activities to undertake in so short a time—often with a fast-changing market to further complicate matters. Any experienced buyer will tell the reader that simply having a 'passion for fashion' is just not enough. Grit, determination, drive, dedication, and empathy are also needed in equal amounts.

Good luck with your career in fashion buying!

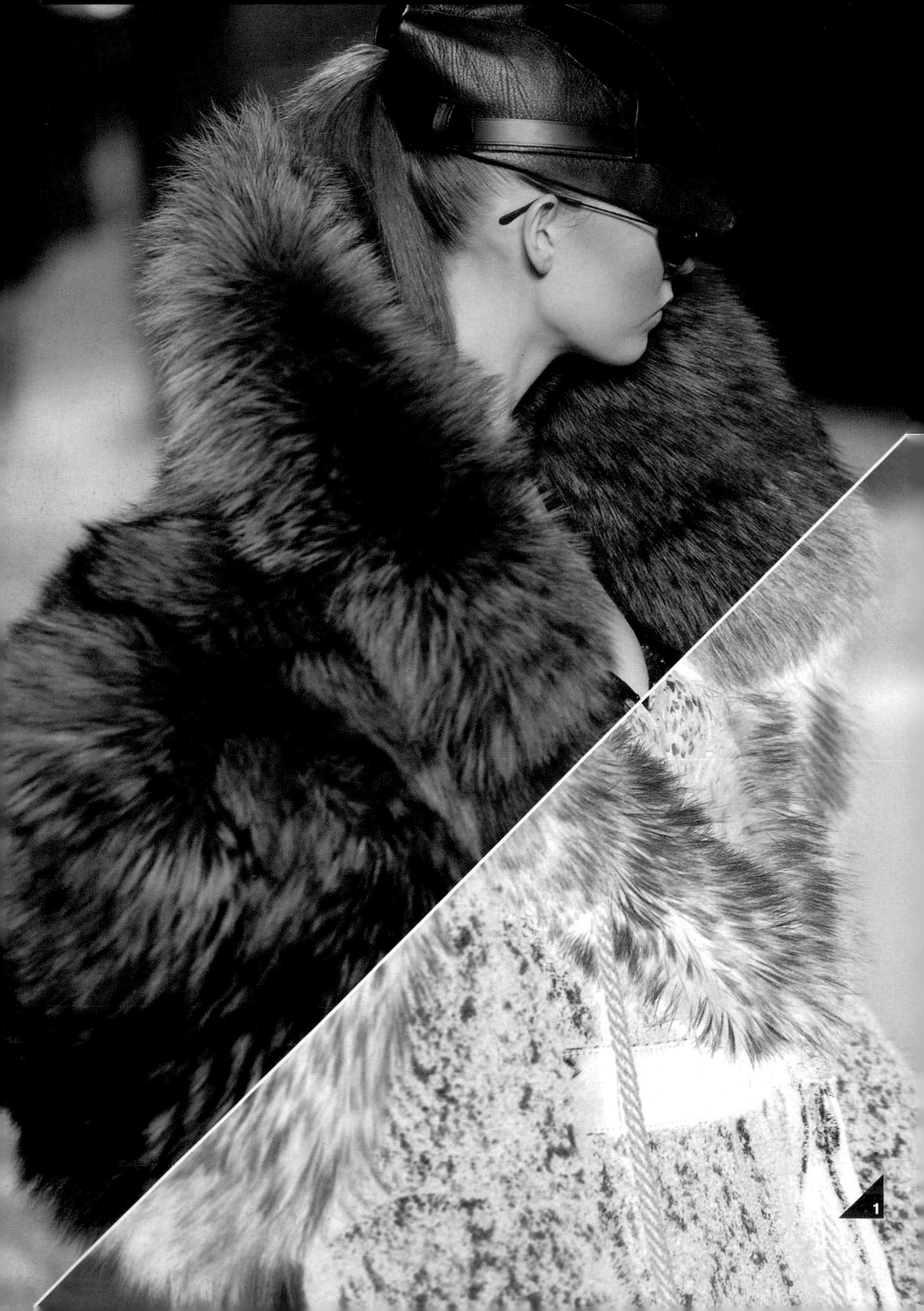
1

THE FASHION BUYER

1

Fashion buying is often seen as being one of the most glamorous of all fashion retailing roles. Many parts of it are; however, other aspects of the job require a business-savvy mind, strong attention to detail, and sheer determination. Fashion buying is a tough, competitive world in which buyers work with all product levels, across different sectors of the industry—from discount operations to the most expensive high-end brands.

How a buyer operates varies considerably: a department store buyer may select from preexisting branded ranges; while a buyer for a mid-range, private-label clothing retailer will be required to develop a unique range from scratch. Whatever the sector, the success of any fashion business relies on the buyer to purchase a unique range of products that both attract customers and generate revenue for the retail organization.

1 AUTUMN/WINTER 2010–11

In Viktor & Rolf's prêt-à-porter fall collection, the duo created avant-garde yet luxurious

What is a fashion buyer?

A fashion buyer is the individual or group of individuals (the buying team) whose primary role is to purchase merchandise for a retail organization. They work diligently in researching trends, sourcing materials and/or product, creating seasonal buying plans and working with outside vendors and designers to produce a range that will be distributed to brick-and-mortar locations, online stores, and catalogs.

Fashion buyers often have more influence over and impact on the overall financial success of a business than do fashion designers themselves. Although designers are the starting point of any fashion product, it is the buyer who will select the final range that they believe has the best opportunity to drive sales for the retail organization; and therefore of also fulfilling the targeted customers' needs and wants.

Three key factors prescribe the scope of the buyer's job description: how the retailer's organization is structured, the size of the retail operation that they are buying for, and product assortment.

Throughout the year, buyers work with designers to continually develop, edit and reject ideas, samples and/or brands from those originally considered, whittling down items for potential inclusion in the final range(s). Whether buying for their own shop or for a large chain, the real acid test of a fashion buyer comes down to seeing if the product selected makes it onto the shop floor and sells out at full retail price.

In reality, a buyer rarely (if ever) achieves a 100 percent success or strike rate. There is always an element of any range that does not sell well and will require a price reduction to help move it out of the shop. This in turn reduces the overall profit level of the business.

2 BUYER CHECKING FOR GARMENT FIT

A buyer and designer work together to inspect garment patterns for fit based on the intended demographic aimed at for the seasonal buying plan.

2

Qualifications and expectations

Fashion buying is a competitive business with applicants coming from a wide variety of educational backgrounds; and many different skills and attributes are required to become a successful fashion buyer. Human resources professionals in the fashion trade are always trying to find the magic formula when recruiting for buying roles: simply having a passion for fashion is not enough.

Internationally, the number of fashion-related, design, manufacturing, buying, marketing and management courses is increasing exponentially. Some have a stronger business focus, while others are more design-related, but none give any applicant automatic entry into a buying job. Your letter of application, a strong CV, personal drive and a convincing interview will often be as important as having a relevant degree. A buyer's role requires an individual to:

× be efficient, flexible, and positive;
× provide a high level of critical thinking;
× work independently and in groups;
× be able to analyze sales trends;
× understand current and foresee future trends across different markets.

"Fashion is not something that exists in dresses only. Fashion is in the sky, in the street; fashion has to do with ideas, the way we live, what is happening."
Coco Chanel

What is a fashion buyer?

Buying teams and their working environment

Usually, a product team consists of four to six people, but there could be more or less depending on the size of the organization. Buying staff work long hours against strict deadlines and are highly profit motivated. The buying team typically comprises of the following key personnel:

× buyer
× assistant buyer
× buying admin assistant
× merchandiser
× assistant merchandiser
× merchandising admin assistant.

Certain product buying teams tend to be larger due to the complexity or importance of the product area concerned, as in the case for accessories and women's tops, for instance.

For large fashion retail shop groups, the buying office may often consist of well in excess of 100 people. However, with staffing costs constantly increasing, most companies continually aim to keep teams lean but efficient.

3 THE BUYING TEAM

A buyer and assistant buyer discuss color swatches in order to prepare new lines for the forthcoming season.

3

For large fashion retail shop groups, the buying office may often consist of well in excess of 100 people. However, with staffing costs constantly increasing, most companies continually aim to keep teams lean but efficient.

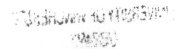

4

KEY SKILLS NEEDED TO BECOME A FASHION BUYER

What makes the perfect buyer is an amalgamation of personal and business skills and attributes, which changes regularly depending upon the business context and the economic environment.

Fashion
On-the-pulse fashion awareness; Ability to anticipate and interpret fashion trends and looks; Strong skills in creating range coordination.

Product
Sound product and technical knowledge.

Physical
Good color vision; Physical and mental agility; High stamina level.

Management
Good written and verbal communication; Decisive; Organized—with excellent time-management skills; Numerate; Professional; Customer-centric; Good negotiator.

Personal
Highly motivated to achieve success; Enthusiastic; Friendly; Firm but fair; Outgoing; Imaginative; Conscientious; Curious; Desire for lifelong learning.

The general state of organization and the atmosphere of a buying office can often be a good indicator as to the overall mood and ethos of a retail business. Buying floors are typically open plan—with each product group separated by hanging garment rails and storage bays. For those buying apparel, body forms are seen close by for garment fit assurance. Well-appointed departments have metal parallel rails or grids fitted to all the spare wall space available. Grids enable complex products and ranges to be hung and viewed together for consideration.

Proper (preferably natural) lighting, large work surfaces (for garment measuring and examination) and spacious conference rooms provide the ideal working conditions for meetings, and for the continual decision making and reflection required by buyers and their team members.

4   INSIDE A BUSY FASHION BUYING OFFICE

Product teams typically work in groups, working well into the night to meet strict deadlines, in preparation for the final range.

What is a fashion buyer?

Working with other retailing roles

The fashion buyer's diary is generally packed with a host of internal meetings. Most buying offices plan weekly, monthly and seasonal meetings well in advance of the season that they are buying for, also taking into account planned foreign buying trips. This is when strong communication with those playing other roles in the organization becomes imperative for a successful (and profitable) seasonal buying plan.

A buyer's good reputation in the trade is important as they act as an ambassador for the business. It is therefore crucial for the fashion buyer to display a consistent, efficient, and friendly demeanor in all their dealings, while at the same time remaining commercial, professional, and firm in all negotiations. The fashion business is more about the people than the product.

Garment technologists

As more fashion products are produced abroad, home technology teams have become smaller. They now act more as a management hub, with remotely based international offices and technologists. Buyers rarely have a technological background or training, so tend to rely heavily on their technologist to give guidance and advice on a wide variety of product suitability, durability, and reliability issues. A good buyer<>technologist relationship is therefore imperative.

All garments and fabrics require testing before release to the consumer, requiring buyers to continually scrutinize, check, and sign off a wide variety of test reports during the course of their work. Attention to detail is vital. Using internationally, nationally and house-recognized product performance standards, buyers and their teams will work with their technologists to ensure that quality assurance standards are maintained.

5 BEING A TEAM PLAYER

A buyer must work with a wide range of colleagues, and act as the go-to intermediary between those in corporate and supplier roles, streamlining and facilitating communication between them.

FASHION BUYER

INTERNAL RELATIONSHIPS

GARMENT
TECHNOLOGISTS
PLANNING/
DISTRIBUTION
MARKETING &
BRANDING
RETAIL STAFF

EXTERNAL RELATIONSHIPS

SUPPLIERS
PRESS AND MEDIA
TRADE BODIES &
ASSOCIATIONS
EDUCATIONAL SYSTEMS
RETAIL STAFF

Planning and distribution

Although these departments tend to deal more with merchandising staff, from time to time fashion buyers inevitably become involved with both. Importing is a complex area and a buyer with a good relationship with this department can often get their merchandise shipped faster and more efficiently. As buyers gain experience, the unique problems of importing unfold—if anything can go wrong it often does, usually with a best-selling line!

Once imported merchandise arrives at the distribution center (DC), it then needs to be moved to the retail outlets as fast as possible. Merchandisers are highly involved with the DC management and team, but again, experienced buyers often visit the DC to ensure that good relationships are maintained.

Marketing and branding

Larger fashion businesses have well-developed marketing and/or branding functions. Some businesses fully integrate the marketing and branding functions into the buying office; others keep them separated. Either way, the personnel involved will rely heavily upon the buying team to provide up to date information about new lines, hot sellers, problems, and other issues of direct concern to them.

Buyers may also provide help with photo shoots, press days, or other external marketing communications, though this is fairly uncommon. However, buyers help themselves, their ranges, and their trading performance by being helpful and available to assist with marketing and branding activities.

Fabric suppliers

Although some buying offices have their own fabric buying team, in smaller businesses without a specialist, the buyer may meet with key fabric suppliers as well as garment suppliers. Keeping abreast of new fabrics and technological advances is an extremely important buying attribute.

Press and media

Buyers are often asked to meet with their retail organization's press, publicity, or media personnel: getting a product into a magazine shoot can greatly increase sales. Buyers should be prepared to talk knowledgeably with their PR staff, which in turn will help them to write up a feature or review (getting a product into a magazine shoot can greatly increase sales). Pre-season press shows are also held to showcase the new ranges to the media, at which buyers will be expected to attend to again talk knowledgeably about the range(s).

Trade bodies/associations and charities

A wide range of trade associations and organizations will approach buyers for help, information and support. Some are legally based, such as trading standards and tax and customs; others are voluntary or socially based, such as trade, national, or locally centered charities. The scope and scale of such requests varies by country. As any long-serving buyer will agree, everybody wants to meet the buyer as they are seen as a pivotal and important point of contact.

Colleges and universities

Buyers are increasingly asked to deliver talks and to support a variety of academic institutions and fashion courses. Many favor their old college or university, although other institutions that provide regular and reliable interns also carry favor.

◀ What is a fashion buyer?   Fashion buying approaches ▶

18

Retail environments and the buyer

The buyer's relationship with retail staff

Having a good rapport with your brick-and-mortar management team is key to successful sell-through. Having well-trained and well-informed selling staff is critical for any successful fashion business: it is therefore imperative for the buyer to have strong and consistent communication between their department and the retail stores. Strong communication between the buying teams and the retail store management teams will foster an environment that simultaneously works to drive sales and to push units per transaction. It is a group collaboration that has one goal—profit.

Seasoned buyers generally spend at least a day or two visiting their retail stores to see their departments and ranges selling in situ. This is most effective during peak trading times, usually designated by the store management team based on sales tracking. For some locations, it could be Friday through to Sunday, while others might have peak sales during the business week lunch hour.

Regardless of peak hours of operation, these visits allow the buyer to see how consumers are reacting to their purchases; they also give retail staff the opportunity to provide valuable feedback on both the successes and perceived new opportunities within the range.

Buyers will also talk with outlet managers to get a top-down view of their products, and will undoubtedly visit competitors to see what new ranges have come in. Some fashion retail businesses make every Friday a store visit day. Buyers who fail to undertake regular branch visits can become very shortsighted about what is really happening in the market and have a tendency to make seasonal buys based on personal instead of consumer needs.

Having well-trained and well-informed selling staff is critical for any successful fashion business. Some businesses therefore send their buying teams on a travelling roadshow around key cities in the country well ahead of the season in order to preview the next season's range to key retail staff—providing them with information such as color stories, fit changes, and new brand launches.

Strong communication between the buying teams and the retail store management teams will foster an environment that simultaneously works to drive sales and to push units per transaction. It is a group collaboration that has one goal—profit.

6

These roadshows are often held in hotels or training rooms and sometimes have a live fashion show as their key attraction. The intention is to train, enthuse and motivate retail staff to sell the next season's range. At such seasonal presentations, senior retail management will also be in attendance to see what the marketing and selling priorities of the season ahead will be.

Most fashion businesses also distribute a weekly newsletter to their stores keeping them informed of problems, promotions, changed priorities and any other issues relating to retail trading. This is especially important when a buyer needs the help of the retail staff to aggressively push SKUs in an attempt to gain the most profit margin from heavy seasonal buys.

Often, buyers and merchandisers are asked to write weekly updates for their department at the start of each week. Items discussed could be RTVs, fit, and/or quality issues. Good internal marketing communication about product ranges (both positive and negative) is a useful way for retailers to stay ahead of their competition.

6 CARRYING OUT QUALITY INSPECTIONS

A buyer reviews some of her range in a retail shop, looking for quality issues and seeing how consumers react to the product in situ.

◀ What is a fashion buyer?   Fashion buying approaches ▶

20

Retail environments and the buyer

Types of retail stores

It is important to remember that the fashion industry is a commercial, for-profit business like any other and it begins and ends with the customer. Research into consumer behavior and spending patterns drives the creation and development of innovative fashion to suit customer needs. Fashion retailers trade in many different formats, from department stores to discount outlets. The fashion buyer must understand the different retail typologies and how retail types operate internationally.

Department stores

These retail types have large-selling square footages and are typically multilevel. They are mostly found in large urban cities, but they have also made their way into suburban malls. Department stores sell a wide range of goods from high fashion to electronics.

There are also specialty department stores that offer a more narrow range of the aforementioned goods. Famous department stores include Selfridges (London), Galeries Lafayette (Paris), and Barney's (New York).

Specialty retailers

These are small-to-large space retailers, which usually form part of a larger shop chain with flagship locations. These retailers may be gender-specific or exclusively market to families (men, women, and children). They trade at various market levels, generally termed low, middle, and high. Low-end examples include Old Navy (USA) and Primark (UK); Gap, Monsoon, J. Crew, Kurt Geiger, Whistles, and Topshop are typical middle-end (internationally); and high-end tend to comprise either locally known or national brands, such as Jaeger (UK), Bally (UK), or Kate Spade (USA).

7
8

7–8 FASHION AT WORK

Fashion retailers target certain demographics based on their retail typology. A department store, such as Harvey Nichols (fig. 7) offers a wide range of assortment for a wide range of consumers, whereas a specialty store such as Urban Outfitters (fig. 8) caters to a niche market offering a more narrow product assortment.

THE CONTINUUM OF CLOTHING AND FASHION

9 THE FASHION
   MARKETPLACE

Fashion is exchanged and
marketed at a range of
levels across society, from
clothes-swap parties held in
domestic homes to the multi-
million pound marketplace
represented by haute couture.

HAUTE COUTURE

LUXURY BRANDS

DESIGNERS

DESIGNER BRANDS

DEPARTMENT STORES

RELATIVE PRICE

HIGH-STREET HIGH FASHION

HIGH-STREET LOW FASHION

OFF-PRICE RETAILERS

DISCOUNTERS

SUPERMARKETS

MARKETS

CHARITY SHOPS

CLOTHES-SWAP PARTIES

LEVELS OF ASPIRATION

9

◀ What is a fashion buyer?　　　　　　　　　　Fashion buying approaches ▶

22

Retail environments and the buyer

Boutiques

Boutiques are typically one to three small retail shops, which are independently owned and operated. They offer a narrow range of specialty goods; predominantly other fashion labels (but sometimes also private labels or custom designs too). Their product is typically more expensive and selectively restocked. At boutiques, the shop owner usually acts as both the manager and buyer.

Discount operations

These big-box retailers are similar to department stores, but they typically sell goods at significantly lower price points. They buy in large quantities in an effort to pass their savings on to consumers. Brands sold here are not viewed as high fashion, but still have strong market following. Well-known discount operations include Tesco in Europe and Target in the USA.

Supermarkets and hypermarkets

Historically, supermarkets and hypermarkets mainly sold food, but in an endeavor to achieve higher profits, many are now stocking their own clothing brands. This movement is particularly strong in the UK and Canadian markets, but is becoming increasingly popular in the USA as well. Joe Fresh for Loblaw in Canada, for example, is a private fashion label that has recently branched out into free standing brick-and-mortar locations in the USA.

Factory outlets and factory village stores

Factory outlets were originally created on factory sites to sell off faulty or excess stock. Today, many upmarket and mid-market brands sell overstock, faulty, and special lines in these more remote retail locations. The large-scale factory village was originally an American concept.

Vintage, charity, or thrift shops

Vintage clothing has now become a key fashion look. Green issues and recycling have been major drivers, along with an increased consumer desire to source unique products. Approximately 7,000 charity shops operate in the UK alone selling pre-worn clothing, and the numbers are spreading globally.

E-tailing

Catalogs have been used to sell fashion extensively over the past 100 years, especially to those people living in remote or rural locations. Catalogs also provided consumer credit before the advent of the credit card. Although still in use, catalogs are now being replaced by electronic trading, or what is known as e-tailing, which offers a convenient way for the consumer to shop from wherever they are based. Retailers are able to reach out to consumer markets across the globe via personal computers, smartphones, and tablets.

Other types of retail outlet

Airports, train stations, hospitals, and large office complexes are now utilizing spare square footage for incorporating different retailer types. Some companies run short-term pop-up shops or home and office selling parties—there really are no boundaries to where fashion can be sold. Additionally, concessions refer to small brands or designers that rent space inside the stores of larger retailers, paying weekly commission (or a contractual amount) on the sales that they have achieved.

10

10 MARKET LEVELS

There are so many different types and market levels of fashion retailing, and each targets its own segment of the market, be it a discount operation, such as T.K. Maxx, or boutiques, department stores, or e-tailing shops.

Retail environments and the buyer

National brands vs. private labels

Fashion retailers either stock products that they have developed and manufactured for themselves, which are generally uniquely sold in their own business (private label buying). Or, they may buy ready-designed existing brands from manufacturers and/ or design houses (national or international brand buying). Retailers such as department stores often sell a combination of the two.

National (or international) brand buying requires the buyer to select which brand names or designers are to be stocked, as well as to select and subedit the individual lines to be stocked or bought from each range. Buying branded merchandise requires the buyer to pick those elements of the branded range that best fit their own business customer profile. This is usually an editing job as, during any given season, few retailers stock all the lines offered by a brand. This type of buying does not normally involve the buyer with the initial development of each branded/ designer range.

11

Branded buying is typically used by both small independent fashion shops and by large department stores, although retailers' profits tend to be lower on this product due to the high cost of brand marketing.

Private label buying, on the other hand, requires a much more creative and original approach than does branded buying. Here, the buyer is involved in assisting designers to create and develop ideas, after which they then select the garments/products suitable for the season's range. Each garment or product is unique, having been initially designed by either an external or an in-house designer or design team. Once lines are selected, it will be the buyer's job to ensure that the best cost price is achieved, the right factory is sourced and a workable delivery date is negotiated.

A retailer's profits tend to be higher on this type of product, as they source bulk deliveries directly from the factory to achieve economies of scale, thus giving the keenest cost price. In many cases, retailers will provide what is known as the "brand is the label," whereby only one brand exists in the retail shop and that label is also used as the company name. This branding type is seen in retailers such as Gap, H&M, and Pink.

12

11–12 NATIONAL AND PRIVATE LABELS

National brands can be seen in specialty or department stores, whereas many retailers have become household brands in their own right—such as H&M.

"We are looking to brands for poetry and for spirituality, because we're not getting those things from our communities or from each other."
Naomi Klein

Fashion buying approaches

The buying cycle – understanding consumer purchasing habits

There are several theories proposed for explaining why consumers purchase in the way that they do. However, most people agree that there are common underlying motives that prompt a consumer to purchase a specific item, which is typically reflected on afterwards. Buyers need to understand these motives, along with other significant theories and approaches to consumer behavior, in order to best capture their intended retail market.

One of the earliest (and most popular) theories of human motivation was proposed in the 1950s by Abraham Maslow, who discussed the idea that individuals move through stages of growth, needing to fulfill each stage before moving to the next. Maslow identified the stages (in order of priority) as: physiological/psychological needs, safety and security, self-esteem, and love and belonging, leading to the desired goal of self-actualization (see fig.13). Buyers can evaluate and gauge which stage their consumer market is in and create a seasonal buying plan and pricing strategy that correlates to it.

Another interesting model is the concept of decision-making theory (see fig. 14), which introduces a holistic approach that can be used to evaluate how consumers purchase goods. Though it is difficult to foresee individual buying choices, buyers can use this model to ensure that their purchases make it from the racks to the register more frequently, as well as for ensuring that issues such as quality, fit, and trend decline don't prevent the mass consumer from keeping the merchandise.

13

SELF-
ACTUALIZATION

SELF-ESTEEM

LOVE AND BELONGING

SAFTEY AND SECURITY

PHYSIOLOGICAL/PSYCHOLOGICAL NEEDS

AWARENESS OF NEED

REFLECTION PERIOD

INFORMATION SEEKING/
RESEARCH

DECISION TO/NOT TO PURCHASE

ASSESSMENT OF ALTERNATIVE/
RISK EVALUATION

Being aware of approaches like the concept of decision-making theory will allow buyers to dig deeper into the mindset of their consumers, which can be used to better understand their own purchasing methodology. Then, buyers can readily gauge whether they should make seasonal range purchases for a fast fashion market (discussed later in this chapter) or choose instead to invest in product of a more classic nature that will continually withstand the zeitgeist, depending on the department that they are purchasing for.

CONSUMER PURCHASING MOTIVES

A strong buyer will be aware of the purchasing behaviors of their shoppers and will work to ensure that they are able to capture their market through a combination of the consumer purchasing motives detailed below.

Rational motives
These lie behind purchases that a consumer can justify as a need rather than a want. These items are rationally purchased and typically comprise everyday necessities. Consumers look at things such as quality, care, warranties, etc.

Emotional motives
Items are purchased based on an emotional response to an event in the consumer's life or by a feeling that a particular product gives them. For example, a woman purchases a new luxury handbag because she received a promotion and wants to fit the part. She doesn't really need the handbag, but excitement and a potential higher salary prompt her to purchase it. These purchases usually provide the feeling of prestige, status, or recognition.

Patronage motives
This is used to describe situations when consumers purchase goods based on personal preferences, such as brand loyalty or customer service. Consumers have a tendency to frequent the same retailers and become attached to them.

13–14 THEORIES IN
FASHION BUYING

Fashion buyers use human behavioral theories to try to better understand their customers, such as Maslow's "Hierarchy of needs" (fig.13) and decision-making theory (fig.14), which have long been studied for insight into the rationale behind consumer buying patterns.

Fashion buying approaches

The global consumer has never been richer or more fashion-savvy than they are today. Fashionable clothing is no longer only for the rich—society has democratized fashion so that it is now within easy reach of nearly everyone. People with style can find fashionable clothes at knockdown prices: fashion is not only achieved by buying expensive branded products. Intelligent fashion buyers therefore closely observe what people around them are wearing during their everyday business and social lives. The street is now where many fashion trends start.

"Fashion changes, but style endures."
Coco Chanel

Understanding consumer markets

Understanding the modern consumer is becoming ever harder for the fashion buyer for numerous reasons, some of which are listed below:

× A wider range of fashion influences exist today, often spread virally by social media.
× There is a media-hyped, ever-increasingly faster demand for change and the new.
× People in developed economies generally have higher levels of disposable income.
× Increased levels of social connectivity between different cultural groups have led to greater levels of fashion awareness and a need to keep abreast of trends.
× Social and peer-group pressure is generated and stoked by popular media commentators which encourages fast-changing trends.
× There has been a macro change from formal to casual dressing across the whole world—even in business.
× Fashion has become generally less gender-specific; androgynous dressing styles have been adopted more by both men and women.
× E-tailing (and the Internet) has opened trade between overseas markets, making global trends more accessible.

15

Fashion buyers need to be fervent watchers of society and changing trends. Much of this type of personal research is informal, although frequently buyers—just like designers—will keep scrapbooks of photos, looks and images to act as continuous sources of buying inspiration that they can later refer back to. It has even been known for buyers for one large fashion retailer to be paid to regularly attend nightclubs to ensure that they are up-to-date with what is being worn in street fashion and subcultures.

The fashion market—along with many other consumer markets—has fragmented as a result of larger social and cultural changes. In Western society today, consumers tend to form style tribes—preferring to create their own look or to be part of smaller trends, rather than merely conforming to mass fashion movements. In the West, trends are generated by a society of individuals; in the East, society as a whole—and especially the family unit—is still highly valued, which has an impact on how fashion is consumed.

Fashion buyers therefore need to be continually aware of societal change and to watch trends and fads as they emerge at an increasingly faster rate. For today's fashion buyer, it has become imperative to understand the needs and wants of much smaller market segments, each of which ceaselessly change and shift in terms of brand allegiance and fashion taste. The day of one-look-for-all fashion is over and the idea of "fast fashion" is becoming more increasingly widespread.

15 STYLE TRIBES

Fashion styles today change at a more accelerated rate than ever before in history. Technology has enabled savvy fashion consumers to be both well-informed and increasingly creative in their personal style choices and fashion purchases.

Fashion buying approaches

Fast fashion explained

The term "just in time" (or JIT) was used as a precursor to the term "fast fashion," which is constantly used by the industry today. It emerged from a Japanese car manufacturing innovation, which shortened the lead time of supply chains, reduced inventory, and made supply very responsive to short-term demand.

There is no official definition of "fast fashion." It simply refers to trying to get the latest runway or other look out onto the shop floor at an affordable price and as fast as possible. Fast fashion is a term used particularly when runway (especially couture) designs are reinterpreted by high-street or mainstream fashion businesses—usually at a fraction of the cost and in a matter of weeks. The idea behind this is that the shorter the lead time it takes to get a garment to the consumer, the less likely it is that competitors will already have a version of the same garment on sale. The fastest competitor to market should in theory reap a quick profit by being the first in—and hopefully out, of a new trend or product line.

Getting in and out of a fashion look quickly is the sign of a good fashion buyer. This is because stocking the latest fashion look for too long, or as demand decreases, can leave a business with too much inventory that may then need to be sold with little or no profit. Most fashion companies therefore aim to continually use quick-response methods to meet consumer demands in order to shorten lead times and improve overall company efficiency.

Undoubtedly, factories, buyers, and logistics managers will need to speed up their reaction rates—and buyers will leave more of their seasonal buy unplanned in order to ensure that they can quickly buy into the next fast fashion look. Fast fashion is becoming increasingly utilized and, for the moment, it is what consumers want.

THE ADVANTAGES OF FAST FASHION FOR THE CUSTOMER

- × Shops change their lines faster—giving consumers more options and thus more choices of things to buy.
- × Lines change so frequently that there is less chance of seeing someone else wearing the same product.
- × The product in shops is always up-to-date and therefore more exciting.
- × Customers are able to buy versions of runway or celebrity-worn products in a matter of days and at significantly more affordable prices.
- × Customers quickly find products that they want to buy—resulting in less frustrating and fewer wasted shopping trips.
- × Consumers get a psychological boost (purchase with emotional motives) from being able to wear what the stars, celebrities, or models are wearing in a simple matter of weeks.

"The turnover of fashion is just so quick and so throwaway, and I think that is a big part of the problem. There is no longevity."
Alexander McQueen

THE FAST FASHION RESPONSE CYCLE

INITIAL CONCEPT/ IDEA SEEN
(e.g. fashion show or celebrity)

PROTOTYPE MADE
(made in any similar fabric)
2 DAYS

FABRIC LOCATED
(maybe own stock fabric or on shelf at supplier + shipped)
2 DAYS

TEXTILE SHIPPED
(+ suitable trimmings)
2–5 DAYS

CLOTHING PRODUCTION
(in pre-booked factory)
3–5 DAYS

GARMENTS SHIPPED
(Europe)
3–5 DAYS
(further distance)
5–7 DAYS

DELIVERED TO DISTRIBUTION CENTER

TRANSPORT TO STORES
2–3 DAYS

ARRIVE IN STORE

SALES
(then move on to a new idea)

CYCLE = 14–24 days
Major variables are:
1. textile availability
2. distance of factory from outlet
3. distance from outlet to shops

16 FAST FASHION CYCLES

The turnaround time for fast fashion is very quick. The time it takes to source, make, and distribute may be faster if a buyer has a good rapport with their vendors than if they do not have strong relationships with their suppliers. The quicker the trending merchandise makes it on to the sales floor, the more likely it will meet projected sales goals.

Fashion buying approaches

Product-specific purchasing

When buyers first enter the industry, most are placed in a department (womenswear, menswear, childrenswear or home goods). They are then typically assigned a product class, such as knits, wovens, accessories, and so on to buy for each season. Womenswear is always the most popular product area for those entering fashion buying, although menswear and childrenswear also offer huge career opportunities and are becoming increasingly more popular, especially in regard to fast fashion.

Women's wardrobes generally contain many more garment types than do those of men or children. Internationally, women tend to spend two to three times more money annually on clothing than do men. There is no clear rationale for this, although the complexity of the female garment and product offer is often cited. In general, all clothing falls into two self-explanatory descriptors—formal or casual. Yet, societal change has created a demand for a far more casual approach to everyday dressing—with casual women's clothing now being accepted as the norm in many business settings.

CLASSIFICATION HIERARCHY OF PRODUCT TYPES

Different businesses, depending mainly on the size of their turnover, may put several product types under one buyer, for example, the jeans and trousers buyer. Similarly, many of the products in accessories are grouped together under one buyer. Every business uses its own classification hierarchy—but, in general, the one detailed below for a dress is typical. Every line will also be given a unique line or lot number for identification and IT purposes.

Gender	Womenswear
Type	Outerwear
Genre	Formal
Department	Dresses
Category	Eveningwear
Sub-category	Long evening dresses
Specific line	One style of evening wear
Size and color	Specific size in specific color/print

17–19 BASIC FEMALE GARMENT TYPES

Though buyers work independently on the specific class of garment that they are in charge of, they often communicate with one another to ensure that the purchases for the season can work interchangeably with all garment types.

Women's wardrobes generally contain many more garment types than do those of men or children. Internationally, women tend to spend two to three times more money annually on clothing than do men.

17 18
19

BASIC FEMALE GARMENT TYPES

Outerwear
Coats, jackets, ponchos, and suiting.

Dresses
A-line, maxi, mini, and onesies.

Tops
Blouses, button-downs, sleeveless, sweaters, T-shirts, and vests.

Bottoms
Skirts, shorts, denim, trousers, culottes/capris, leggings, and jeggings.

Accessories
Bags, belts, scarves, gloves, jewelry, hats, sunglasses, shoes, hosiery, and fashionable technology accessories.

Intimates
Nightwear, underwear, and swimwear.

Fashion buying approaches

Menswear

Menswear has far fewer different product types than does womenswear. Internationally, the formal tailored suit has given way to more casual dressing. Unlike women's fashion buying, men's fashions tend to be less extreme. The three main types of menswear are, however, essentially similar to those of womenswear, and consist of outerwear, accessories, and underwear.

Home goods/lifestyle accessories

Retailers are increasingly investing in lifestyle products for consumers, selling them alongside fashion apparel items. Buyers are quickly learning how these products parallel the fashion industry. Consumers today are rarely seen without their tablets or smartphones. With the traditional business office virtually obsolete these days, we are seeing a greater trend of lifestyle accessories and small home goods in retail shops; from laptop cases to fashionable headphones.

BASIC MALE GARMENT TYPES

Outerwear
Suiting, coats, hoodies and jackets, trousers, jeans, shorts, and shirts.

Tops
Button-downs, T-shirts, sweaters, sweatshirts, and vests.

Bottoms
Denim, sports pants, trousers, and shorts.

Accessories
Gloves, hats, scarves, belts, backpacks, ties, socks, jewelry, sunglasses, and fashionable technology accessories.

Underwear
Loungewear, underwear, and swimwear.

20

20 MENSWEAR

Menswear today has become much less formal and more casual, creating the need for buyers to source and purchase more fashionable items, such as activewear.

21

Childrenswear

Childrenswear is probably the most complex, but least financially lucrative buying area of all. Babies, toddlers, young children, preteens, and teenagers all have different wardrobes. Children's products are sold using various combinations of size, age, and height.

21 HOME GOODS/ LIFESTYLE ACCESS

Many retailers today are incorporating home goods and small accessories in their shops, creating the idea of lifestyle shopping, as in this Fabrice LeRouge store, pictured.

22

22 CHILDRENSWEAR

Childrenswear is a complex product area, which often replicates what adults wear—and can be equally priced.

Retailers are increasingly investing in lifestyle products for consumers, selling them alongside fashion apparel items. Buyers are quickly learning how these products parallel the fashion industry.

Case study: Kristen Lucio, e-commerce entrepreneur

23

Kristen Lucio, fashion stylist turned entrepreneur, owns and operates e-tail boutiques KroweNYC and BadlandsVintage, via the shopping platform Etsy, focusing on a curated collection of vintage apparel and accessories geared toward young adults with a love for unique clothes and a fashion-forward sense of style.

As a stylist, Kristen Lucio has worked as a fashion editor for a Miami-based magazine, had several editorial photo shoots published in various publications, and has also acted as a personal stylist to celebrities. She is currently working on developing an e-commerce site where she will sell modern fashion and accessories from upcoming designers paired with her current vintage collections. Kristen operates both her women's and men's sites and photography studio from her studio in Brooklyn, New York office.

Kristen began her fashion career as a visual merchandiser for a major retail chain, giving her the opportunity to implement corporate art direction, balance budgets, analyze business, and forecast trends. While working as a visual merchandiser, Kristen was consistently building new displays, designing seasonal floor changes and outfitting mannequins.

From there, she was recruited by a fashion stylist to work at the local modeling agency as an assistant. Soon after, she began assisting top stylists who worked on runway shows, major catalogs, and publications, including *Vogue Italia*.

Within a few years, Kristen began working on major television and motion picture films as a costumer and designer in Miami, where she also started to develop a celebrity client base as a personal stylist and shopper for red carpet events and editorial shoots. This gave her experience of calling showrooms and designers to request specific pieces to match the needs of the job.

After deciding to start her own retail shop, Kristen moved to New York City and opened her two online shops, quickly educating herself on various ways to promote, advertise, and sell her product in the rapidly evolving cyber-based shopping community.

Of her new venture, Kristen declares, "This is probably the hardest decision I have made in my career, to open a store – especially one online." Although you might think that it would be easier and cheaper than having a brick-and-mortar store, Kristen would beg to differ: "Quite possibly, it's more difficult. As a start-up, I was the buyer, site merchandiser, social media director, customer service and shipment manager, photographer, stylist and art director simultaneously."

Kristen's advice to any would-be entrepreneur is therefore sanguine: "If you are not feeling passionate about your career choice, then my advice is that you change it – because it's that passion that takes your business to the next level and drives success."

23 KROWENYC

Kristen Lucio is a well-rounded entrepreneur who wears many hats— but her favorite is that of fashion buyer!

Case study: Kristen Lucio, e-commerce entrepreneur

Shop Sections

Shop home   35 iter

SMALL   4

MEDIUM   8

LARGE   14

X LARGE   4

SHOES   2

ACCESSORIES   2

Shop Owner

Krowe
Brooklyn, NY, United States

Contact

Favorites

Followers: 12

Feedback: 3, 100%

Shop Info

☏ BadlandsVtg
Opened on Dec 14, 2(

24 GLOBAL EXPOSURE

Purchasing goods for e-commerce can be a difficult task. Being aware of international trends is a must when live sites can be seen by the global community.

BadlandsVtg
Vintage apparel, accessories and man cave decor

✓ Like 170

Welcome to the Badlands! We look high and low for Men's vintage fashion so you don't have to.

This shop accepts Etsy Gift Cards.

Search in this shop   **Search**   Sort by: Custom ▼

990s Mens Brown Four Poc...
BadlandsVtg $29.00 USD

1980s Samsonite Canvas an...
BadlandsVtg $38.00 USD

1990s Mens Vintage Brooks ...
BadlandsVtg $36.00 USD

1970s Ivory wool knit "Nieuw...
BadlandsVtg $42.00 USD

1980s Taupe Hounds tooth ...

1980s Mens NY Yankees Bo...

Mr. Rogers 1970s Sky Blue ...

1980s Classic Trench coat w...

24

Interview: Kristen Lucio

Q **How do you source your buying range?**

A My inventory originally started out from my personal closet and stock from my stylist kit, which was a mishmash of various funky items. Currently, I go on cross-country buying trips and curate a "look" for my shop. My buying advice is: don't over-buy, find out who your customer is and what sells best at what price point, then you will begin to develop a consistency in your aesthetic, as well as in your customer following and sales.

Q **What is your method for sourcing trends for future seasons?**

A People in Los Angeles dress EXTREMELY differently from people in New York so, for example, if you try to buy for and/or merchandise your store with New York trends, your customers in L.A. are less likely to make a purchase because they don't understand the east coast market trends. Years ago, I would rely on fashion magazines and www.style.com for current runway trends but now, social media and blogs make it so easy—and at times overwhelming—to find out what's happening in fashion trends all over the world.

"People in Los Angeles dress EXTREMELY differently from people in New York so, for example, if you try to buy for and/or merchandise your store with New York trends, your customers in L.A. are less likely to make a purchase because they don't understand the east coast market trends."

Q **What will typically prompt the sale or promotion of an item?**

A I see people do sales according to season but I don't follow that trend because on the Internet, everything is in season somewhere! I'll do promotions that will get me more subscribers/followers, however, so I get return customers through these sorts of promotions: "Follow us on Twitter/Facebook and get 15% off your purchase." Social media is great for this line of advertising.

Q **Has e-commerce impacted the demand for your product?**

A I would say it has catapulted vintage into the forefront of Internet shopping. Although the competition is high, you would have previously had to depend solely on foot traffic to make sales, since your inventory is all one of a kind; so, advertising was not really an option to display or promote your products.

Q **Having worked in visual merchandising, do you now feel that buyers and the store's visual team should have a direct relationship?**

A When I worked in visual merchandising, I would definitely reach out to the buyers when I felt it was necessary. I definitely think that buyers are trained to purchase and drive the store business and to successfully do that, product needs to be displayed or outfitted in a way to maximize the sales of that particular stores customer. So the merchandiser needs to sometimes break away from the company's visual mold and do what is best for their environment.

Q **How do you determine pricing for your garments?**

A I don't have a specific "percent" with which I mark up the clothes. I research what other vintage sellers are pricing similar items at and usually price garments competitively from there. It's important to make sure that you are making enough profit to pay for labor and the cost of other things needed for the business, like laundering used items, photo shoots, etc.

Chapter 1 summary

This chapter has examined the importance of the buyer to a business or company in terms of their fundamental profit-making role. It has also explored the personal attributes and skills that make up the ideal buyer. The fashion buyer's role within the team is explained and the ways in which the work differs for branded goods and own-label buyers is explored. The wider range of womenswear and menswear has been discussed, and the huge range of issues of childrenswear touched upon. We have also explored the many different types of retail businesses where fashion buyers may work—and discovered that not all fashion buying is top end and high design.

Questions and discussion points

Having looked at what makes a successful fashion buyer and how and where they work in today's competitive marketplace, here are a few questions for you to consider further.

1. Do you think that you already possess some of the key skills and attributes needed to be a successful buyer?

2. Which of the skills and attributes do you feel you would like to learn more about and why?

3. Do you think that buying womenswear is easier than buying menswear or childrenswear?

4. When considering the difference between buying branded goods from existing brand/designer ranges or working with suppliers and designers to create a unique own-label range, which type of buying would be more personally satisfying to you and why?

5. Do you think that fashion can only be bought in high-end designer and high-market level shops?

6. What types of stores do you personally like to shop in and why?

Exercises

1. Rank the skills and attributes indicated in Chapter 1 in order of importance as if you were responsible for recruiting a buyer for a fashion business catering for trendy 16- to 22-year-old female customers. List the reasons for your choice(s).

2. Undertake a trip with friends to your favorite shopping area and see if you can find examples of the different types of fashion/clothing shops described in Chapter 1. Write down as many names as you can under each shop type.

3. Repeat question 2 for shops of the opposite gender – do you find this a harder task? Why might this be?

4. Using the list you generated from answering question 2, now note down how many of these businesses you do not visit regularly. Write a comment against each of these explaining why you do not shop here and compare your list with that of your friends.

5. Go into a large department store and talk to shop sales staff – ask them to tell you about brands that you may never have heard of. During your conversations with them, find out which of these lines are own-label, branded/designer or concession. See if you can find at least two examples of each.

6. Together with friends, choose your favorite three fashion shops and write a few short sentences explaining what makes them so good. Is it the shop, the stock, the staff and/or other factors that please you most?

7. Try to locate and visit a vintage/pre-worn shop or charity/thrift shop and list the description of items (if any) that you would consider buying and wearing. If none, explain your reasons why not in a written statement.

2

SOURCES OF BUYING INSPIRATION

Fashions have changed throughout history, sometimes radically. Previously, people tried to copy the styles of aristocrats or royalty and fashion ideas were transmitted internationally by wealthy travelers visiting foreign lands. Fashion magazines, such as *American Vogue*, illustrated with line drawings and later photographs, were the first mass tools of fashion communication.

Cinema and TV became important conduits for the transference of international fashion ideas between the 1930s–1950s; French, Italian, and particularly American films had huge global influence. The Internet has fulfilled this role since the 1990s.

Now that we can transmit ideas electronically across the globe in seconds, fashion trends spread faster than ever before. This has complicated the work of fashion buyers, who today have to work ever faster to receive, synthesize, develop, and process fashion trends—before eventually converting them into the look of the moment as best-selling topical fashion.

1 SPRING/SUMMER 2011

Zac Posen's prêt-à-porter womenswear accentuated the fun aspect of feathers and bows, with Posen stating: "It's important to dress as you believe and to enjoy fashion too... So many people are following fashion now. It's becoming fashion-tainment."

Buyers, designers and markets

International market similarities and differences

A buyer will be faced with many challenges, but the greatest one by far is trying to create a seasonal range for both domestic and international markets. Retailers who invest in overseas markets will typically create buying teams for both national and international home office locations, ensuring that the target market is accurately reached in those locations.

At first, it can be tricky to learn the lexicon associated with different markets and positions within those markets. In the USA, for example, a head or senior buyer may also act as the merchandising manager for a gender, class, department, or more. In addition, the term "merchandiser" increasingly refers to the person who oversees the allocation and distribution of product assortments, as well as also overseeing visual merchandising strategies (the creation of artistic displays to enhance the promotion and sale of goods).

In both instances, the key factor is that the head buyer and merchandiser are essentially working to ensure the successful sale of their product. However, it is worth bearing in mind that the terms' meanings vary and/or can be used interchangeably depending on the retail organization that you are working for and the country that you are stationed in.

2

Another significant difference at play that buyers need to be aware of is the falling and rising of market values. If a buyer is providing seasonal ranges for both domestic and international markets, they should be aware of financial issues that may affect the price of their goods being sold, such as whether one currency is worth more than that of another. Buyers should be aware of the ways in which market economies can dictate the pricing strategies for goods sold overseas. If the price point is consistent and does not take into account international market fluctuation, an organization's profit could turn out to be much lower than anticipated.

Other factors that may Impede upon a buyer's ability to do their job successfully are elements such as lead times for samples or product, or for any other information that needs to travel from one country to another. Knowing if international markets impose taxes or tariffs on goods brought either into or out of your country is also vital.

Fortunately, buyers are easily able to investigate these things on the Internet and address any issues prior to them occurring: widespread use of the Internet has helped to close much of the gap once seen between domestic and international retail markets. Being aware of international events is imperative for the buyer who wants to stay ahead of the competition.

INTERNATIONAL TRADE ASSOCIATES THAT WILL PROVIDE A BUYER WITH MARKET INSIGHT

Fashion Group International
An authority on all things business relating to fashion and retail design. They provide individuals and companies with tools, thus enabling them to become more expert in their field.
fgi.org

VMSD
Retail design, merchandising, product knowledge, and industry news are their forte.
vmsd.com

RDI
The Retail Design Institute promotes the advancement of and collaboration with retail environments.
retaildesigninstitute.org

FIRAE
The forum for International Retail Association Executives advocates and promotes the exchange of market information among international retail trade associations.
firae.org

POPAI
A global retail trade association that provides education and research for marketing in the retail industry.
popai.com

2 INTRODUCING PRODUCT TO NEW MARKETS

At the International Market for Retail Real Estate (MAPIC), a retail buyer investigates a vendor's product line. Such events introduce new product and suppliers to existing markets with the prospect for global expansion.

Buyers, designers, and markets

It is often wrongly presumed that "fashion" means expensive, and that fashion buying by extension involves buying high-end products. In reality, fashion buyers are employed at all levels of the market place, largely due to the democratization of fashion that has occurred as a result of expanding markets.

Stylish fashion is no longer solely the preserve of the wealthy, nor is it only available when buying high-priced products. Fashionable merchandise is increasingly available at all levels of the market and today, people who have a strong sense of style can afford to dress very fashionably on a budget. Simply wearing an expensive brand or designer label no longer automatically makes a person fashionable.

This phenomenon is sometimes called *the "Primark to Prada effect*," which refers both to the fact that consumers are increasingly savvy about new trends emerging at the high-end of the market; and to endeavors by more mainstream or high-street brands to emulate and reproduce these trends in the form of more affordable garments.

3–4 FROM PRIMARK TO PRADA

The stripped-back aesthetic of this store shop front for the international retailer Primark presents a very different brand offer to that of the luxurious opulence of Prada—one of vast choice, contemporary trends and pared-back price points—the keystones of its runaway success.

3
4

Trickle-down theory

Trickle-up theory

highest social bracket

DIRECTION OF FASHION CHANGE

MAJOR VARIABLES ARE:

1. INITIATING SOURCE
2. FASHION CHANGE DIRECTION

3. FREQUENCY/SPEED OF CHANGE
4. CHANGE DYNAMICS

lowest social bracket

Trickle-across theory

5

5 **DIRECTIONAL FASHION CHANGE THEORY**

In some cases, a trickle-across effect may occur whereby all subcultures adopt a trend simultaneously and rapidly. This typically results from the convergence of mass media channels.

Buyers will also look at directional theories of fashion change to understand how markets are influenced across varying consumer segments and, in particular, to discover who started it, where it is heading, and how long the fashion trend will last. A trend may be introduced at the higher end of the market but then be later translated and adopted at a more affordable price, by the lower end of the market (or vice versa). It is precisely this availability of fashion in a wider range of retail stores and the cross-fertilization between market sectors that has directly resulted in the creation of many new fashion buying jobs.

THE FASHION BUYER'S MANTRA

VALUE ∝ QUALITY × PRICE

At all market levels customers increasingly expect value for their money, whether they are buying fashion in a discount shop or from a couture house. The key equation to remember here is that value ∝ quality × price (value is proportional to the relationship between quality and price).

Buyers, designers and markets

The fashion designer< >buyer relationship

The fashion designer<>buyer relationship is very close—however, it is ultimately the buyer who makes the final decisions and takes responsibility for putting products into the range.

Most large fashion retailers and brands now employ their own design team. The way in which design and buying teams are structured varies from business to business, but normally each product buyer will have a designer assigned to help them with the development of ideas and samples.

On the other hand, many smaller fashion businesses do not have enough turnover to justify employing full-time designers, often preferring to hire project or range-specific freelancers. The benefit of using freelance designers is that a fresh eye will create each new product and/or range: if a sole designer or buyer works for too long on a product area or brand, they can easily become creatively stagnant.

6 DESIGNERS<>BUYERS

Fashion buyers work closely together with designers in the development of each season's range. Most ideas start as a two-dimensional drawing before later being developed into a prototype sample.

7

Many months ahead of the buying season, the whole team of buyers and designers, regardless of whether they are internal or external, will meet to discuss the new trends and future directions of the total business. During these early stages, preliminary brainstorming is used, alongside externally generated trend forecasts provided by commissioned out-of-house trend forecasting agencies. Inspiration comes from all parties involved, but primarily from the buyer and designer who will work together to project the greatest profit achievable from forecasted trends.

7 WORKING WITH DESIGNERS

Designers make adjustments based on suggestions from their retail buyer. These designers are contract workers, based out of an external office.

Market research

Buyers are expected to undertake continuous market research using both informal and formal research techniques, as well as qualitative and quantitative data. Informal sources of information are gathered through conversations with colleagues and friends both within and outside the buyer's own organization.

Business meetings with external parties may provide buyers with inside information about their competitors and the trade in general. Often, such information can be used to the business's own advantage. However, it is important to remain an ethical business practitioner: be mindful that some insights provided about your competitors should remain with the external parties providing them.

The marketing mix

The concept of marketing is often ill-understood by people in and outside of the fashion business, with many believing it is simply about using PR and advertising. In fact, marketing involves so much more than this—it is about everything that the company (and especially the buyer) does to create product, as well as to provide service and value for its customers; who in turn purchase the product and hopefully remain loyal to it through repeat purchases.

Good marketing is ultimately about creating long-term customer relationships. Professor Neil H. Borden of Harvard Business School drew upon this basic premise to come up with what he called the "marketing mix" in 1948. This basic marketing concept proposes that all good marketing is about placing the right product in the right place at the right price and then giving it the right promotion.

THE BUYER'S DILEMMA

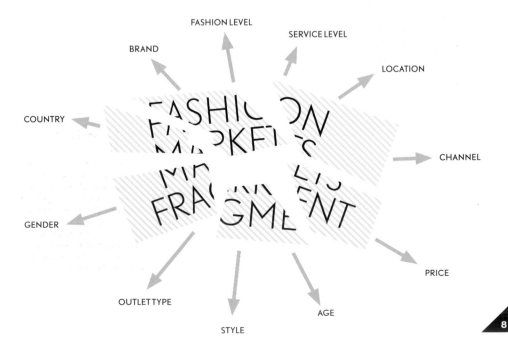

FASHION LEVEL

BRAND

SERVICE LEVEL

LOCATION

COUNTRY

CHANNEL

GENDER

FASHION MARKETS MINI FRAGMENT

PRICE

OUTLET TYPE

AGE

STYLE

8

Although this might appear fairly simple, getting all four aspects right in fashion marketing is not quite as easy as it sounds. Fashion buyers would generally not describe themselves as pure marketers, although they are in fact the main drivers of, and have the greatest influence on, the marketing mix of any fashion business. It is the fashion buyer who defines the product, has a major input into the retail pricing strategies, decides (in conjunction with the merchandiser) which outlets the products will be stocked in and finally provides important input into any associated promotional activity.

Formal market research

The media shows a great interest in all things related to the fashion business and fashion business stories are covered in the business section of many international newspapers, such as the Wall Street Journal (USA) or Financial Times (UK). Buyers need to read these sources of media in order to be aware of financial and business matters concerning their competitors.

In addition to keeping abreast of the business and fashion news, many buyers may also have a dedicated marketing research manager who will help them to synthesize information with regular market updates—most probably using some of the regular marketing research reports that are available.

INTERNATIONAL MARKET REPORTS

Mintel
Providers of a wide range of international fashion reports; this is a paid service that is available in printed or electronic format. These reports are often available through academic libraries.
mintel.com/press-centre/press-releases/category/2/fashion

Verdict
Focusing on retail, Verdict provides a range of international fashion-related reports. Used mainly by companies.
verdict.co.uk/reports_sector.htm

Euromonitor
Euromonitor is a very internationally focused service that covers many business sectors, including fashion.
euromonitor.com

Key Note
UK-centric in focus, yet with a wide offer of clothing reports.
keynote.co.uk/index

NB: There are many other specialist research companies operating—reports often typically focus on one country's fashion market.

8 FASHION MARKETS FRAGMENT

Buyers are constantly faced with various market fragments that can weaken the brand image and cause marketing to become insignificant. Using strong intuition combined with quantitative and qualitative data provided by both internal and external sources can help to strengthen a retailer's brand through the seasonal buys.

Market research

Focus on the customer

Buyers who believe that their own good taste is more important than that of their customers invariably fail. The best fashion buyers have an innate ability to absorb huge amounts of data and information, which they then use to underpin their buying decisions. This data comes from demographic and/ or psychographic studies conducted either internally or externally.

The level of marketing research undertaken by different fashion companies varies enormously. Some businesses may recruit small groups from their targeted audience (focus groups) to undertake semi-structured research into their opinions, attitudes, brand preferences and buying habits.

Other companies, depending upon the size of the organization, may take data that has been collected by a professional marketing research or brand consultancy firm. This ensures that a business always understands its customers or potential customer base and supports their final decisions when planning a new range, providing a total picture of the new products that their targeted customers both want and need.

"I design for real people. I think of our customers all the time. There is no virtue whatsoever in creating clothing or accessories that are not practical."
Giorgio Armani

10

Facts and figures about quantitative market trends

Demographic and psychographic data about spend per capita, broken down by gender, age, brand, and so on, is often made available to buyers in order to help them to understand key socioeconomic trends. Past, current, and projected sales performance is regularly reviewed, often on a daily or weekly basis to help the buyer understand what is selling well or not. This supports decisions such as buying more or reducing prices.

This is also an area in which retail shops within the company can provide additional information regarding their customers, in order to either reiterate what the home office and buying teams already know, or to provide insights into changes occurring in their specific market place.

Sales associates are influenced by their everyday lives and the cultural environment surrounding them—music, popular culture, media, street fashion—all have an impact. This type of informal market research is essential in helping the buyer to understand how their customers dress.

9

UNDERSTANDING A RETAILER'S CONSUMER SEGMENTATION

Listed here is a range of marketing strategies that a buyer will typically use to further understand their consumer base.

Psychographics—a combination of both demographics and psychology that looks at consumer behavior, values and preferences.

Target audience—a segment of the consumer population identified by both demographics and psychographics, which enable a buyer to gain insights into the tangible and intangible attributes of a company's image, services, and/or products.

Differentiation—presents a company's image, services, and/or product in a way to best showcase their leading edge over others in their category.

Positioning—a marketing approach that uses target audience and differentiation to create a niche market for a retailer's brand, goods or services.

9–10 UNDERSTANDING YOUR CUSTOMER BASE

Buyers look at their consumer segment, which provides demographic characteristics such as gender, age, ethnicity, and income, to put together a customer profile associated with a specific retailer.

Trend forecasting

Structured trend forecasting dates back to the 1970s, although fashion designers, manufacturers, and buyers always undertook their own informal research long before this. Trend forecasting is an increasingly important function as getting fashion trends wrong is an expensive business; poor-selling stock requires prices to be reduced thus reducing company profit.

Concepts, color, and sources

The way in which each buyer assimilates trends has some commonality across different types of business. Many larger companies do this in a more ordered way, with smaller businesses being likely to take a more ad hoc approach. Larger companies are also more able to afford the services of relatively expensive external trend forecasting agencies.

Most fashion buyers will use a combination of trend forecasting sources when deciding on a new range. They may use one of the leading French trend forecasting agencies, such as Peclers, or the increasingly influential UK-based Worth Global Style Network (WGSN) or Stylesight, for example. Most offer basic and more expensive custom-made trend forecasting services and can provide forecasts for many seasons ahead. These are delivered either online or in a physical trend/lookbook format. The trend books carry clear color illustrations, fabric swatches or hanks of yarn, which are useful when discussing and developing ranges with a supplier.

11–12 COLOR FORECASTING

Many buyers will look at color forecasting agencies such as Pantone, whose famous PMS (Pantone Matching System) is used for a wide variety of mediums from paper to fabric. Pantone's brand has become a leader in color forecasting and is highly respected in the fashion industry, often collaborating with retailers— as seen below with Uniqlo's cashmere collection.

11 12

THE DIFFUSION CURVE

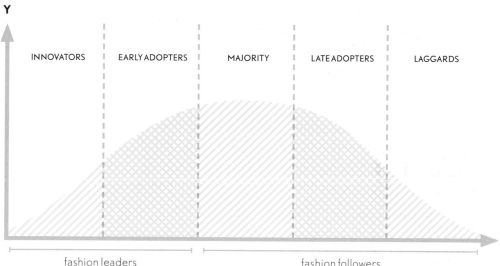

13

Like anyone working in fashion, a fashion buyer is subject to a variety of other trend influences, be these from an individual's personal life, meetings with colleagues, manufacturers, management, or the wider fashion media. Some newer fashion companies will even pay for young buyers to attend clubs, music festivals, and venues. Throughout the year, buyers will also attend a variety of international fashion fairs, shows, and exhibitions, as well as taking foreign shopping research trips. Generally traveling with a designer, buyers will start to take notes and pictures to help them determine the direction of their future range, a process that leads to obtaining more formal marketing research.

13 DIFFUSION OF INNOVATION

Everette Rodgers introduced the idea of fashion diffusion in the 1960s. He stated that innovation needed to be presented to the public for approval and/or adoption. The amount of time (X) it takes for this new innovation to be filtered through the population of consumers (Y) is the innovation life cycle. Buyers can use this theory to trend forecast the potential duration of a seasonal range.

Trend forecasting

The number of specialist trade events available for international fashion buyers to attend is expanding exponentially. Buyers working with larger fashion businesses will plan their attendance carefully, attending only those shows that are directly relevant to their product ranges or in an effort to see the most innovative product.

14–16 INTERNATIONAL TRADE SHOWS AND FAIRS

Buyers normally expect to visit only a few key shows or fairs each season—many are specialist and product-specific. There are many vendors at these shows and they all hope to entice the buyer to choose their range as the next season's range.

Trade exhibitions, fairs, and shows

Buyers often attend shows with other buyers, in-house designers (and/or designers of their manufacturers), and occasionally with senior management. Trade exhibitions are spread over many kilometers of space, often involving hundreds of booths for vendors, manufacturers, suppliers, etc. "Doing a show" in a random, unplanned format can prove both a waste of time and money, for all parties involved.

In a fast-changing market such as fashion, buyers often find that they spend far too long in the office, dealing with administration, the buying team, and making endless phone calls to suppliers. Trade exhibitions therefore allow buyers thinking time and the ability to be inspired by the industry, constantly taking notes on those products that have great sales potential.

14

15
16

WHY TRADE SHOWS AND FAIRS ARE SO IMPORTANT FOR FASHION BUYERS

Spending money and time at trade events must deliver direct benefit to the business, while enabling fashion buyers to:

× Stay abreast of the latest developments and ranges of existing and new suppliers, brands, or designers
× Gather new ideas to help develop future ranges
× Network with other people, organizations, and business to ensure currency of own thinking and ideas
× Find new potential suppliers, brands, or designers not currently used
× Confirm that the ranges already developed and developing in the business are still relevant to the forthcoming season(s)
× Potentially place orders —mainly for those buyers in smaller or independent businesses that buy designer and manufacturer brands.

"I don't think women need another black bag. Everybody has a black bag already, so I thought this season (needs) colour."
Carolina Herrera

Trend forecasting

Many stands will have products that may not be directly relevant to the buyer, but that will nevertheless enable them to encounter a new shade, texture, style, or print that will create ideas for potential use in the future.

Buyers and designers sketch garments or details that are new and innovative or take photographs as they wander around an exhibition: well-organized buyers keep copious notes of show visits, along with relevant business cards and brochures from events. Note that sometimes using a camera is not permitted and so it may be worth checking with the show's organizers first.

17
18

17–18 EXHIBITION VENDORS

Vendors create visually appealing booths in the hope of attracting the next big retailer. Since exhibition space is not cheap, vendors will pay a hefty price tag for a booth that is close to entry/exit points and on corners or aisles.

No buyer can visit every stand, nor is it logical to visit existing suppliers who regularly visit head office. It is essential to obtain a show or exhibition plan as soon as you arrive and to mark up and plan visits, mainly to new or potentially exciting stands.

Even with planning, the unexpected is likely to occur, such as when a new or exciting unseen brand or manufacturer is encountered for the first time. Often, buyers will aim to help each other out by noting interesting things that they see during the day and exchanging notes with each other later in the evening.

19

Doing the shops

Since most fashion exhibitions and shows are held in the fashion capitals of the world, it is normal for buyers to also take time out to "do the shops." Undertaking comparative shopping trips, in an effort to discover new or previously undiscovered brands and shops, can yield a plethora of ideas for future development. Most large businesses will allow buyers to take or purchase important or innovative products that they find, in order for these items to then be later shown at the buying offices.

Comparative shopping trips, like visiting trade fairs, need to be carefully structured. Often, trend forecasting agencies will be able to provide buyers with a list of the hottest shops and shopping areas ahead of a foreign trip, on request. Being out and about in a fashionable city also provides opportunities to spot new trends bubbling up at street-level. This is also a great opportunity to begin the market research phase needed to introduce new brands to a retailer through the season's buying range.

20

19–20 GLOBAL SHOPPING EXCURSIONS

Buyers will occasionally get the opportunity to venture overseas and visit up-and-coming markets in search of new brand opportunities or design inspiration, such as the Kantao Region (top) in Japan or the city markets of Ephesus, Turkey (below).

Trend forecasting

Fashion weeks, trade fairs, and exhibitions are held biannually to enable designers and branded manufacturers of fiber, yarn, and fabric—as well as garment manufacturers—to exhibit their next season's range to international buyers. They are generally held in January, February, and March, and September, October, and November to respectively showcase the following autumn/winter and spring/summer ranges.

21 INTERNATIONAL FASHION SHOWS

Buyers attend the F/W 2013 David Jones season launch for designer Dion Lee. Buyers at small retailers often look to larger organizations to ensure that their product range aligns with those bigger footprints in the industry.

Fiber, yarn, and fabric fairs

Fiber, yarn, and fabric fairs are always the first in the cycle—and take place at least a year ahead of the garment season. Own-label buyers would be more likely to attend such fairs than would branded buyers.

Key yarn fairs are Pitti Filati in Florence and Expofil in Paris. Key textile and fabric fairs are Indigo and Première Vision in Paris, Tissu Premier in Lille, Moda In in Milan and Inter Textile in Shanghai. Chinese and Indian fairs will no doubt significantly increase in importance over the next decade.

International fashion weeks

The main cities influencing international fashion are Paris for womenswear and Milan for menswear. The other important international fashion weeks are those held in New York, Tokyo and London—although debate rages each season as to which is the most influential. There are many more countries now also putting on fashion weeks—the list increases every year.

Fashion weeks are made up largely of a combination of runway shows and static exhibitions, with events usually spread across cities in a variety of prestigious locations. They tend to attract the smaller independent and boutique buyer, as well as a varied coterie of other fashionistas, bloggers, and industry figures, including the international fashion press. Buyers from larger retail organizations buying branded and designer lines might also be in attendance and own-label buyers are occasional attendees.

"It's a new era in fashion – there are no rules. It's all about the individual and personal style, wearing high-end, low-end, classic labels, and up-and-coming designers all together."
Alexander McQueen

International ready-to-wear trade fairs

These biannual events are generally held in large exhibition halls or on specialist trade exhibition sites. They typically consist of static stands with displays, with some fashion being shown on live models.

Generally running for four to five days, they attract a wide audience with both independent/small-store buyers attending alongside buyers from the larger groups.

Key fairs and cities include Prêt a Porter in Paris, CPD in Düssledorf, MAGIC in Las Vegas, ISF in Tokyo, Pitti Uomo, Pitti Bimbo and Modaprima in Florence, and Pure in London.

Some shows specialize in one product, some are unisex, or focus solely on childrenswear, while others aim to attract younger and edgier buyers. These shows attract brand manufacturers from all over the world, although some aim to attract more home producers.

Smaller businesses will actually place orders at these shows, while larger own-label buyers will undertake research, probably having placed production and orders much earlier with unbranded manufacturers. It is worth keeping in mind that a large proportion of the world's factories produce solely for own-label buyers and would not be represented at this type of fair.

Trend forecasting

1 North America

Mercedes-Benz Fashion Week
New York City, New York

Bridal Fashion Week
New York City, New York

Los Angeles Fashion Week
Los Angeles, California

World Mastercard Fashion Week
Toronto, Ontario

Mercedes-Benz Fashion Week
Mexico City, Mexico

2 Europe

Milano Menswear (Moda Uomo)
Milan, Italy

Ethical Fashion Show
Berlin, Germany

London Fashion Week
London, United Kingdom

Barcelona Bridal Week
Barcelona, Spain

Stockholm Fashion Week
Stockholm, Sweden

3 Asia

Hong Kong Fashion Week
Hong Kong, Hong Kong

Wills Lifestyle India Fashion Week
New Delhi, India

Mercedes-Benz Fashion Week
Tokyo, Japan

Seoul Fashion Week
Seoul, South Korea

Shanghai Fashion Week
Shangahi, China

4 South America

Senac-Rio Fashion Week
Rio De Janeiro, Brazil

Columbiatex de las Americas
Medellín, Colombia

Trinidad & Tobago Fashion Week
Port of Spain, Trinidad & Tobago

Fashion Rio
Rio de Janeiro, Brazil

Buenos Aires Fashion Week
Buenos Aires, Argentina

3

22 INTERNATIONAL FASHION EVENTS AND DATES

There are many key events in the annual fashion calendar which take place all over the world. Buyers should familiarize themselves with these events and attend those that are most applicable for their work.

5

5 Africa

Fashion at Design Indaba
Cape Town, South Africa

Mercedes-Benz Fashion Week
Johannesburg, South Africa

Fashion Week Tunisia
Carthage, Tunisia

Dubai Fashion Week
Dubai, United Arab Emirates

The Hub of Africa Fashion Week
Addis Ababa, Ethiopia

6 South Pacific

L'Oréal Melbourne Fashion Week
Melbourne, Australia

iD Dunnedin Fashion Week
Dunnedin, New Zealand

Philippines Fashion Week
Pasay, Philippines

Rosemount Sydney Fashion Festival
Sydney, Australia

Men's Fashion Week
Singapore, Singapore

6

22

Case study: Promostyl

Trend forecasting is a vital investment that enables retailers to accurately gauge what their customers are looking for in current and future seasons. It represents a big investment—but is one that potentially results in big profits, too! Although there are now many trend consultancies operating, Promostyl was one of the first to become established, having actively provided major trend forecasts in fashion, beauty, design, decor, and beauty since the 1960s. Today, Promostyl have over 30 agencies across the globe, their main offices being located in New York, Paris, and Tokyo.

LINGERIE TRENDBOOK /// WINTER 13/14

THEME 1 : ENFANCES

The recreational world of childhood is expressed in colorblocks, games and inventories... for a fanciful yet structured lingerie.

PROMO**STYL**

PREVIEW /// LINGERIE **24**

Promostyl "interprets emerging lifestyle movements, mentalities and cultural trends" through elements such as color, shape, print, and textiles. Using methods such as observations, interviews, and environmental scanning, forecasters at Promostyl are able to sense cultural drifts that indicate where society may be heading in terms of fashion and design. This information enables retailers, and specifically buyers, to formulate a strategic window in which to successfully create product for their consumers and in which consumers are encouraged to adopt the product.

23-24 A LEADING TREND FORECASTER

Promostyl provides trend forecasting and consultancy services around the globe through its international offices and a user-friendly website (promostyl.com).

Case study: Promostyl

Promostyl is a client-oriented agency that helps deliver sales results through our personalized tailor-made projects.

OUR METHOD   OUR EXPERTISE   OUR CLIENTS

25 TREND DELIVERY

Promostyl's clients can utilize their product in various ways, from web-based inspiration guides to tangible packs uniquely created for the firm. Each method provides professional and thoroughly researched information to assist buyers with future range purchasing.

PROMO**STYL** & **PRINT**S○URCE

Style Guide Spring /Summer 2012

P O L Y C H R O M Y

POLYCHROMY:
We awaken the senses with a techno-edge theme
focused on the postive energy of light and color.
An emphasis on electric and glitter effects boost the
basics and infuse new life into casualwear. The
palette is made up of bright tones that are offset
by intense neutrals to form lyrical and dissonant
harmonies. The print direction takes classic prints
and infuses them with saturated colors and
overlapping 3D effects.

25

Interview: Matthew Jeatt

Matthew is the Director of Promostyl in London, UK. He left college with a music career firmly in his sights and soon became tour manager for many famous music acts including Duran Duran, Meat Loaf, Gladys Knight, and Stan Getz. He then entered the fashion industry. Although he claims not to be a creative, he loves music and fashion—two industries rich with new ideas and trends, and industries in which he thrived using his astute powers of observation and attention to detail. He is one of the most well-respected trend forecasters in the business today; a man with a unique ability to look, see, think, forecast, and explain both contemporary culture and the future of fashion.

Q Why has Promostyl remained one of the most important trend forecasting houses in the world? What makes it so successful?

A We are authentic and we maintain our strong opinions—we do not simply offer a reportage service as do many online trend forecasters.

Q Has trend forecasting become more widely used by a greater range of fashion retailers and brands? If so, why?

A A majority of large fashion businesses now have their own in-house trend forecasting specialist or department. Everyone is acknowledging the need for trend forecasting—the scale of operation simply varies. Businesses are definitely using trend forecasting more thoughtfully.

Q How much influence do trend forecasting services have on fashion buying/the fashion buyer?

A Well, buyers tend to look back to try and repeat successes from the past, whereas designers want the new. We particularly help buyers especially to understand how colors evolve from season to season—they really find that aspect helpful.

Q Do you think fashion buyers are using trend forecasting enough or in the right way? How could it be improved?

A Our generic information is essentially not for buyers, but we do offer a much more tailored forecasting service, which buyers find helps them to be more specific about actual looks and colors relative to their business for a particular season.

Q How has the online impacted upon trend forecasting and how have trend forecasters had to react to these changes?

A 'Online' is a meaningless word—it can mainly be used in two ways; either to simply say, "Hello, we're here," or to perform a functional need, such as selling product or providing information. Some forecasters still provide only trend books, others offer a total online delivery, while some use a combination of both.

Q Can trend forecasting be of use to fast fashion retailers? If so, how?

A Yes and they do use it. The speed of take up—or when they come into our cycle—varies. Often, the fast fashion companies will buy our furthest future trend books (24 months on) to look for elements they can use 12 months ahead—they are just compressing the normal cycle.

Q Have the seasonal timelines of trend forecasting changed—for example, have cycles got shorter or faster?

A Despite the onset of fast fashion, they have not changed that much. The old 18–24 months' cycle from planning to manufacturing still applies, but now our clients also need to be able to be responsive to the demands of fast fashion. Promostyl assists our clients to react to trends in the short, medium, and long term.

"At its heart, trend forecasting is all about knowing what the few are doing, understanding it and translating it before the many are doing it."

Chapter 2 summary

This chapter has examined the sources of both formal and informal trend information that buyers draw on in order to develop their future ranges. The increasing use of trend forecasting services has occurred as a result of the Internet, which has enabled ideas and images to be globally transmitted in an instant. There is, of course, no magic formula to trend forecasting that ensures that all the lines selected will become best-selling lines. Ultimately, it all comes down to the skill and ingenuity of the buyer who is responsible for reviewing, synthesizing, and then interpreting the huge amounts of both formal and informal trend information available to them. Buyers should not simply look at things around them—they should see them as well!

Questions and discussion points

Being a good fashion buyer requires a high level of visual literacy and good color vision acuity. Buyers need to be able to look at hundreds of fabric swatches, garments, and ranges, and successfully synthesize information, such as style details, about them. Buyers then use this information to develop future ranges with designers and manufacturers. Successful buyers necessarily develop strong observational awareness and recall.

1. There are many similarities and differences within the international buying market. Based on your country of residence, think about the similarities and differences that exist between foreign markets and your own. Provide a list that clearly defines each and make note on why these similarities or differences may occur.

2. Thinking about *the Primark to Prada effect*, identify a luxury or mid-to-low market trend that shortly afterwards trended in the opposite market. What is the trend? Which market did it start in? Why and how do you think it crossed over?

3. Buyers need to be aware of trends happening in various social brackets. Where can buyers become informed about future, past, and present trends within those social brackets? Provide the social bracket and outlet for obtaining trend research and forecasts.

Exercises

1. Get together with a group of friends and visit your favorite fashion store. Once you get there, head for a range, brand, or product that you personally like and know well. While there, spend no more than ten minutes looking at it. Then, leave the store and write a page of notes about your visit in a notebook. See how much information you can instantly recall—do you remember, for instance, the sizes, processes, fabrics, brand names, colors, or styles of the key items in the range?

2. On your way into work, college, or university, see if you can remember any of the clothes that a fellow passenger or pedestrian was wearing in detail. See if you can recall colors, fabrics, shapes, and accessories; then, think about why you remembered that particular person's clothes. Were they unique or different in some way, or were they in keeping with a particular trend prevalent among a certain age group or sector of society? Write a half-page report explaining what made you recall this person and their style.

3. Think back over the past week about the fashion encounters that you have experienced and then aim to list as many of these as possible. An 'encounter' can refer to seeing fashion in any media, or while out shopping or meeting with friends—in fact, any situation in which you noticed fashion in some shape or form.

4. Visit your local high street and write a brief one-page report entitled: "This season's main fashion looks, fabrics and colors are...." Use a heading for each section and include sketches, swatches, or magazine cuttings to flesh out the information.

5. Using any old recent magazines or newspapers that you have to hand (and that are no longer needed), cut out key pictures that best sum up the main looks of the season. Try to produce your own simple trendboard, showing the three main trends of the season, along with the key colors. Mount these on paper or board, then try talking about them to your friends—this is good practice as buyers always have to be able to explain looks using trend- and moodboards.

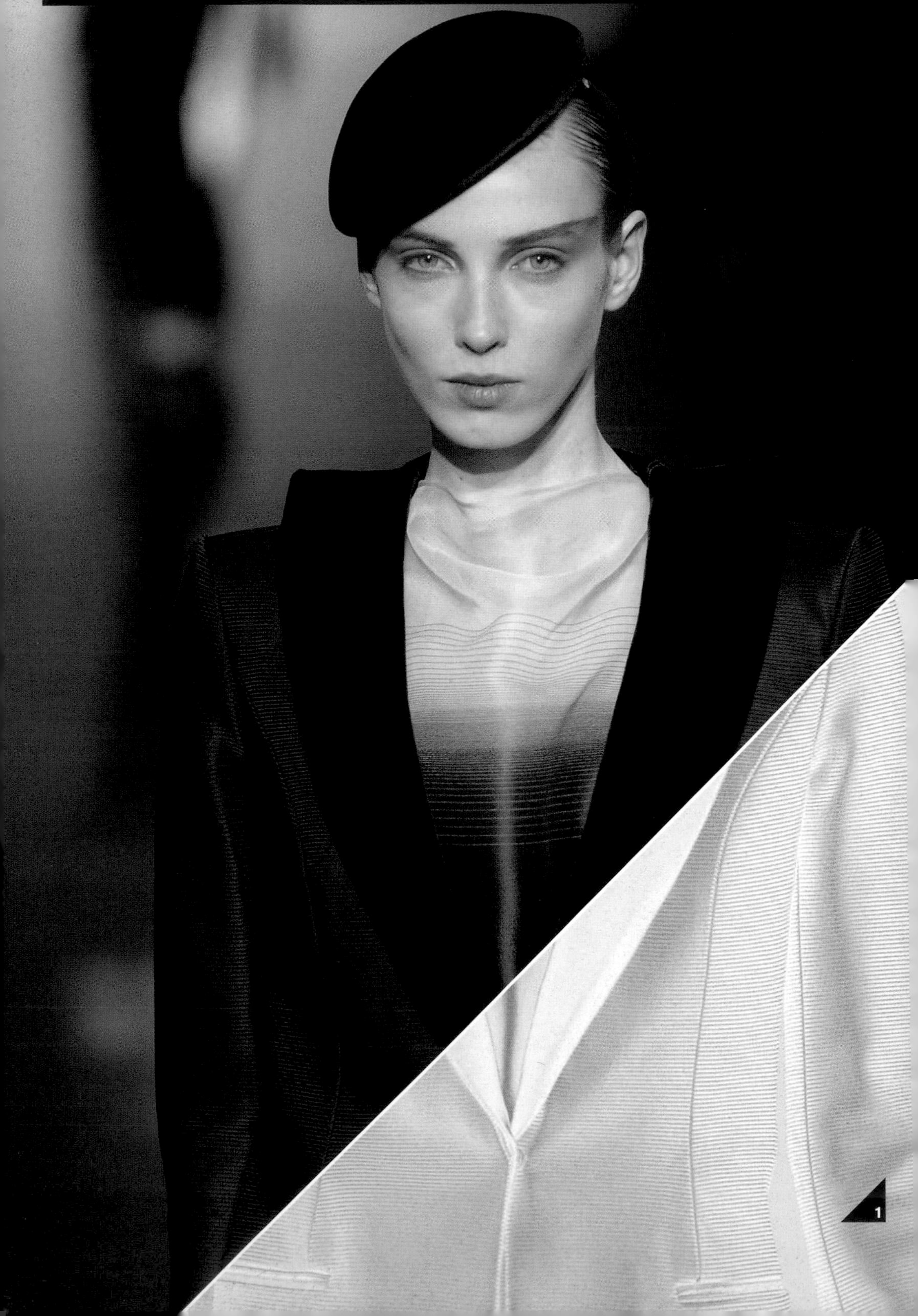
1

3

SUPPLIERS, SOURCING, AND COMMUNICATION

In this chapter, we will examine the all-important buyer<>supplier relationship, exploring how to manage suppliers and their performance within the context of a changing global supply structure. The chapter provides an overview of how buyers go about managing categories and how they progress towards their final-line selection. The perennial problem of sourcing suppliers who engage in sustainable practices is also discussed.

The pivotal communication role of the buyer, in terms of the business's relationship with both internal departments and external agencies, is clarified and reinforced. Finally, we take a look at textile science and the need for buyers to be aware of its importance is emphasized.

1   AUTUMN/WINTER
    2010

Giorgio Armani/Armani Privé
haute couture, seemingly
inspired by art deco line
and form.

What is a supply chain?

A supply chain is a set of firms that make and distribute goods and services to consumers. The length and complexity of the manufacturer-to-retailer supply chain varies dramatically according to market level and product construction. As fabric and garment manufacturing moved away from the developed countries of the West, to the developing nations of the East, many lead times have increased. Depending on the type of fabric and garment construction involved, delivery lead times can be anywhere from three weeks to six months (and sometimes more).

Fashion supply chains involve the cooperation of many individuals, departments, and organizations that are not under the direct control of the fashion buyer. As a general rule, fashion retail businesses do not typically own the complete retail supply chain, but maintain strategic business alliances with each of its members.

The buyer's role in the supply chain

In all fashion businesses—even in those that choose to employ their own in-house design team—it is the buyer who makes the final decision as to whether or not a line is put forward for inclusion into the business's product range. It is the fashion buyer's job to select the product that is most likely to sell at a specified price at a predetermined time to the business's targeted customer base. Many people, functions, organizations, and departments are affected by the buyer's final selection—posing an incredible responsibility for any employee—but the ability to get this right is also one of the most respected attributes of the job.

RETAIL SUPPLY CHANNELS

MANUFACTURER

Manufacturers convert raw goods to fibers, spin/dye yarns and either sell to wholesalers or work with buyers directly on product specifics.

WHOLESALER

Wholesalers store goods in large quantities, to be later sold or distributed to retailers. Discounted rates are often provided for bulk buys.

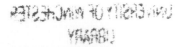

This important decision has an impact on the entire supply chain. From the fabric and garment producers who quickly go into action buying materials and planning their future production schedules, to the retailer's department teams, who plan product assortment, marketing, and promotional incentives for their stores. Regardless of where one fits in the retail supply chain, it is the buyer who sets the course for many of its key players.

THE FASHION SUPPLY CHAIN

Most retailers act solely as the distributor of personal goods to the consumer. However, one notable exception to this rule is the Spanish company Inditex; owner of such famous brands as Zara, Zara Home, Pull & Bear, Massimo Dutti, Bershka, Stradivarius, Oysho, Uterque, and Tempe. This company directly owns and controls a significant proportion of both its textile and garment supply chain.

Other fashion retailers, such as the Arcadia group (formerly the Burton Group Plc), which includes Topshop, Dorothy Perkins, Miss Selfridge and Evans, completely divested themselves of manufacturing capacity many years ago.

When a firm engages in service integration, they are performing multiple activities within the supply chain channel. There are three types of service integration that can occur in this process:

1 Vertical integration—when a company performs more than one activity within the supply chain.
2 Forward integration—when a manufacturer provides both wholesale and retail operations.
3 Backward integration—when a retailer provides wholesale and/or manufacturing services (typically limited services provided).

2   Each supplier has a specific role (sometimes multiple roles) within the system, but each supplier's goal is to provide the consumer with goods and services, even if the consumer is the wholesaler or retailer.

RETAILER

Retailers distribute goods to consumers for personal use. Shops showcase the product range developed by the buyer.

CONSUMER

2

The buyer<>supplier relationship

There are thousands of suppliers and brands available to international fashion buyers— so selecting the right supplier is as (if not more) important than selecting the best-selling fashion look. Having a good supplier base and strong supplier relationships is a necessity for the professional fashion buyer.

Choosing a supplier

Getting the supply and demand for fashion ranges in perfect equilibrium is more difficult than it is for any other type of consumer product. Fashion buyers therefore have a great deal to consider when working with suppliers, especially when introducing new ones.

In the past, buyers were more able to introduce or drop suppliers without much management interference or intervention; but in the competitive fashion business environment, getting the right supply base is imperative and trusting relationships can take a long time to cultivate.

This is why new suppliers are normally required to go through a formalized vetting process, to ensure that their production standards fully meet both internationally required and company-specific quality assurance criteria. The supplier's credit rating is also usually investigated at the same time. Once all aspects of a new supplier's performance have been fully vetted and checked, the supplier can then become an 'approved supplier'.

3 MEETING THE SUPPLIER

Selecting the right supplier is as important as selecting the next best-selling fashion look, in order to ensure that the quality of product is up to par for both retailer and consumers.

Working with local representatives

Suppliers, despite usually having a manufacturing plant thousands of miles away, will generally employ a local representative who is available to liaise with the buyer or other members of the buying team. This is invaluable as most manufacturing units are now located in various international time zones. This representative also acts as the communicator between supplier and retailer, buffering both supplier and retailer frustrations with one another.

3

The advent of the Internet has also revolutionized buyer<>supplier communication, allowing for a quicker exchange of data, information, and images, as well as external conference calling. Some buying offices are linked to key manufacturing plants with high-definition television (HDTV) so that even minute product details can be discussed and alterations made, making business for both parties cheaper and more efficient.

These seamless links between supplier and buyer ensure greater accuracy of production, enabling suppliers to discuss any emergent issues with product directly with the retailer. Reacting quickly can save both the manufacturer and retailer significant amounts of money in production costs that may not have been caught so easily without the use of technology or a field representative.

◀ What is a supply chain?   Managing the supply base ▶

80

The buyer<>supplier relationship

Meeting suppliers

The reception areas of buying offices are busy places, with an ever-changing mix of suppliers and staff stopping to chat and exchange products and information. Suppliers continually drop off samples at the front desk; a collection job for young buying assistants. The flow of garments back and forth to the supplier can seem never-ending, as alterations, changes, and fit adjustments are made.

Again, there are no set rules—the nature of the product, type of supplier, and the specific problem or issue are generally the drivers of meeting demand. That said, good suppliers always tend to have fewer meetings than do bad suppliers!

How buyers and suppliers work together

Experienced fashion buyers always say that although they are forever being approached by new potential supply sources, good suppliers are nevertheless in short supply. Working successfully with any supplier requires the development of a strong and effective business relationship.

Though buyers and suppliers work very closely together, it is probably best that buyers and suppliers try not to develop too close a friendship (of any description) but rather simply maintain a good professional association. This allows for objective rather than emotional business judgment to prevail when stressful situations arise.

4

5

KEY QUALITIES TO LOOK FOR IN A SUPPLIER'S REPRESENTATIVE

As with personal relationships, business relationships come under pressure from time to time—no relationship is ever perfect. Ideally, a fashion buyer seeks the following key personal qualities from a supplier's representative:

× Ability to take and act upon all instructions in an effective and efficient manner
× Good, consistent, and accurate written, verbal, and electronic communication skills
× Creativity in interpretation relating to sample development in terms of line, range and product category
× A consistent and level temperament that remains cool under pressure
× Confidentiality—ability to keep commercially sensitive secrets from competitors and the trade in general
× Good level of technical expertise and the ability to solve construction or quality issues
× Honesty in all dealings—delivery dates, prices, issues, problems – everything to do with the business relationship
× Overall personal efficiency—always does what they say will be done.

In many businesses, fashion buyers are obliged to reveal gifts or lavish entertaining provided by suppliers in order to ensure that their business decision making is objective and not biased by corruption. Retired buyers will confirm that few of their once strong business friendships continue once they no longer control an annual buying budget within the retail sector. Most retailers today will not allow buyers to accept gifts from suppliers in an effort to prevent them from succumbing to the temptation of purchasing product that may not be in the company's best interest.

4–5 WORKING WITH SUPPLIERS

Working successfully with suppliers requires developing strong and effective business relationships where honesty is maintained in all dealings.

Managing the supply base

Buyers are continually being approached by new prospective suppliers. These can be manufacturers, brand owners, or agents— all want to get new business. Most fashion buyers working for large businesses do not have carte blanche to introduce new suppliers without good reason. There is a continual need for buyers to meet and review potential new suppliers, even though a buyer will often meet with many more new suppliers than they could ever possibly need. This is informal marketing research—a vital part of the buyer's role.

Suppliers come to a buyer's attention via a wide variety of sources:

× Word-of-mouth recommendation by a third party—especially fellow buyers or sourcing executives
× Direct approach by new suppliers
× Via trade magazines or articles
× Management suggestion
× Trade attachés of a foreign embassy
× The Internet
× Attendance of foreign trade shows or exhibitions.

QUALITATIVE PERFORMANCE CRITERIA

During the course of planning a season's range, buyers will review each supplier's trading performance including the key criteria outlined here:

× High levels of fashion innovation and design investment meaning better customer focus and thus higher potential profit from having better-selling products.
× General efficiency of entire trading operation. Good selling and design staff will result in a better level of cooperation and communication and thus potentially higher profits.
× Adherence to responsible ethical trading standards set by buyer's organization and international law. Failure to do so may result in adverse publicity and potential loss of customers and profit.
× The organization's manufacturing meets accepted and approved quality standards set by the buying organization, resulting in low product failure rate.

QUANTITATIVE PERFORMANCE CRITERIA

× The amount of stock the supplier delivers versus the percentage that was sold at full price. (Suppliers who need high levels of price reductions will mean less profit for the company.)
× The quantity of poor quality and faulty goods returns that have occurred will result in less profit due to loss of sales.
× Number of deliveries that arrived late, meaning lost profit due to missed sales.
× Value of stock remaining unsold at the end of the season which will result in future potential lost profit due to probable future price reductions.
× Speed to market—fast delivery of new fashion trends will result in higher profits and customers obtaining the latest looks.

Monitoring supplier performance

A good buyer<>supplier relationship can last for years but sometimes it can last for just one season. No supplier is ever guaranteed business if their merchandise fails to sell. Merchandise reporting systems use sophisticated ranking and weighing reports to highlight problem suppliers.

At all times, buyers and their senior managers will look to drop poor performing suppliers in order to replace them with newer and hopefully better ones. Buyers will recommend new suppliers, who generally have to go through an official approval process before being accepted as mainstream suppliers. For small test buys, these standards can be relaxed for the purpose of commerciality and speed.

Buyers are continually under management pressure to reduce the number of suppliers that they deal with in order to:

× Achieve economies of scale by buying more from fewer suppliers
× Make business administration simpler
× Improve the buyers' own time management
× Make buying decision making less complicated.

Buyers are continually under pressure to reduce the number of suppliers that they deal with, in an effort to achieve economies of scale and simplify processes.

Sourcing issues

Fashion buyers always need to keep abreast of global manufacturing shifts. The growth of specialist sourcing departments and experts working alongside fashion buyers has occurred as a result of the seismic garment and textile manufacturing shifts that took place after the advent of World War II.

In much of the developed world, fashion clothing prices have declined in real terms over the past two decades as a result of consumers becoming used to buying fashion at very low prices. Fashion buyers have target profit margins and they are always trying to negotiate the best value for their business. However, chasing low prices alone can be dangerous and may simply lead to the development of a mediocre fashion range.

Manufacturing cheap clothing

To date, technology has been unable to replace human hand-sewing skills. Due to the high number of techniques that are irreplaceable by machine, garment manufacturing has inevitably shifted toward the cheapest producing nations. Yet, there are also downsides to producing cheap clothing and potentially grave environmental consequences for both the people and the countries that manufacture fast fashion product.

LOWER FASHION PRICES =

POSITIVE
- × IMPROVED AND MORE EFFICIENT SHIPPING AND LOGISTICS
- × THE DEVELOPMENT OF LOW OVERHEAD RETAIL OPERATORS—FOR EXAMPLE DISCOUNTERS
- × GREATER EMPHASIS ON DIRECT DEALING BETWEEN MANUFACTURERS AND RETAILERS RESULTING IN FEWER AGENTS OR MIDDLEMEN
- × OVERALL INCREASE IN DEMAND FOR FASHION AS WESTERN CONSUMERS BECOME WEALTHIER

NEGATIVE
- × CUSTOMERS WEARING CHEAP CLOTHING A FEW TIMES AND THEN DISPOSING OF IT WHICH LEADS TO POLLUTION AND WASTE
- × MID-MARKET RETAIL CHAIN FINDING IT HARD TO COMPETE ON PRICE RESULTING IN CLOSURES, JOB LOSSES, AND REDUCTION OF PROFITABILITY
- × CONSUMERS WEANED AWAY FROM QUALITY CLOTHING THAT LASTS SO THAT QUALITY AND STYLE DRIFT DOWN TO BASIC LEVEL

Economic history shows that countries with cheap labor output eventually become more expensive, as workers' living standards rise. There is even evidence in relatively cheap markets, such as India, of what is referred to as "a race to the bottom," whereby manufacturers have been known to move to even cheaper countries as a way of reducing costs.

Global sourcing

Each area of the globe provides potential opportunities to produce quality, low-cost fashion goods. The biggest growing areas of concern facing retailers today are international labor laws and competitive worker wages which should be investigated prior to securing deals with overseas suppliers.

Asia and India

The key garment producing areas that are currently growing fast are China, India, Sri Lanka, and Bangladesh. Other interesting areas enjoying growth are Cambodia, Thailand, Vietnam, and Tibet. Clothing production in these countries always tends to migrate to neighboring countries that have a plentiful supply of cheap and readily available labor.

Western Europe

Textile and garment manufacturing in Western Europe is under pressure due to higher labor costs, especially in the UK, France, Germany, Belgium, the Netherlands, Portugal, and Italy. Where the fashion industry remains in these countries, it is generally very high quality, high design, high value, and/or high tech; or it is used for simple fast-response products. Often, cheaper end production takes place in Europe using illegal immigrant labor.

Eastern Europe

Turkey is an important garment-producing area, with other Eastern European countries, such as Cyprus, Hungary, Bulgaria, and Romania also manufacturing clothing. Again, these countries have suffered from the price competition characteristic of cheaper Asian and Indian production.

Africa and Middle East

Africa is the continent with probably the greatest future. South Africa represents the continent's largest manufacturing nation; but manufacturing has also developed in several North African countries (and former colonial outposts), notably Algeria, Morocco, and Tunisia. In the future, Africa is likely to become the largest garment and textile producing area—it has an abundance of unemployed labor which in turn can potentially provide low-cost labor. Some specialist garment manufacturing units operate in Middle Eastern countries, such as Syria, Egypt, and Israel; all face price competition from China.

The Americas

North America's once large textile and garment industry was originally based around the cotton producing southern states, but has declined like those of Europe. A large and thriving garment manufacturing industry subsequently developed across the border in Mexico which is still important and thriving today.

6 THE PRICE OF FASHION

While retailers strive to maintain low prices for consumers, they can underestimate the negative side effects of doing business in this manner.

Sourcing issues

7 GLOBAL SOURCING

Garment manufacturing has shifted towards the cheapest producing nations due to the high number of techniques that are irreplaceable by machine—but there are potential social and environmental downsides for those countries that manufacture fast fashion ranges to developed nations.

7

Developing product categories and selecting lines

Buyers are forever considering future seasonal buys and will be thinking and assembling ideas for color, style, and/or brand offer well ahead of the actual point of purchasing. They will have their initial ideas turned into first samples runs and/or purchase samples during visits to foreign shops. Merchandisers will have previously worked with the buyer to decide how many line options, colors, and sizes will be needed to fill the next season's buying plan for each product category.

Choosing product categories

The first key part of the buying operation will be to decide which product categories need to be developed and bought first. Obviously, those with longer lead times (for example, knitwear) need to be given priority over simpler, quick-lead-time products such as cut-and-sewn cotton tops.

Buyers will have decided during the early forecasting/merchandise planning phase as to which product categories are likely to be in growth or decline, or to be "on-" or "off-trend" for the upcoming season. Buyers and designers will have had meetings regarding trends, possibly taking guidance from trend forecasting services. However, nothing is guaranteed and this part of the buying process is where the experienced buyer brings into play their ability to synthesize a multitude of information to produce the right category balance.

Selecting lines

The next stage in the process is to select the actual lines that make up each category. First, the buyer should consider what the line offer will look like in small shops compared to in large ones. The small shop range is always the hardest to decide upon, as there are so few options with which to satisfy overall customer demand and space for product is often limited.

Buyers always have too many sample lines available in relation to the final number that will be bought and delivered to the shops. The buyer continually edits out lines until arriving at the final selection. The final selection process is undertaken over time by the team as a whole including the buying assistants. A process of discussion and reflection between buyer and merchandiser is therefore critical during this process. From here, buyers will begin to look at fiber, yarn, and textile selections that will be used for the final selected range.

SELECTING THE RIGHT SUPPLIER TO DEVELOP PRODUCT LINES

Although the cost price of fabric and garments is a key consideration for all types of fashion buying, negotiating the cheapest price is not always the most important objective. Fashion buyers also seek a range of other assurances when sourcing suppliers.

Product quality
Will the supplier (manufacturer or brand) deliver a product that meets the business's predefined quality standards—will it wear, wash, and last? No buyer wants customer returns!

Product delivery
Can the supplier make the product in time for it to be delivered for the planned selling period?

Product fashion level
Can the supplier efficiently interpret the fashion required? Does the brand offer the right level of fashionability? Supplier creativity is very important.

Communication efficiency
Does the supplier maintain regular communication at all times with the buyer and their key support team?

Compatible personality
Does the supplier representative work well and get on with the buyer?

Ethically managed production
Does the supplier manage its own sourcing and manufacturing ethically? For example, the United Nations via UNICEF sets rules determining the suggested age for young people to start work in a factory—this is usually from the age of 16.

8   AUTUMN/WINTER
    2010–11

Dolce & Gabbana's prêt-à-porter menswear collection was inspired by a simple workwear aesthetic, characterized by cut-and-sewn cotton T-shirt tops—quick lead time products that can be rapidly manufactured.

Fabric selection

Color, fabric ideas, and trends are the starting point of all fashion buying. In Chapter 2, we explored the way in which trends and trend forecasting are employed in buying decision making. Once the style or 'look' of a range of garments has been decided upon, fabric selection is usually one of the earliest buying calendar decisions to be made. It involves careful thought and planning in relation to the garments to be created and appropriate selection from the range of fabrics available to the buyer.

Fiber types

Fabrics are made up of either natural fibers that come from animals or plants (such as wool or cotton) or man-made fibers, which are typically made from mineral or synthetic-based chemical substances (such as acrylic or polyester). Often, several types of synthetic and natural fibres are woven together to create fabrics with a better appearance, hand or functional properties.

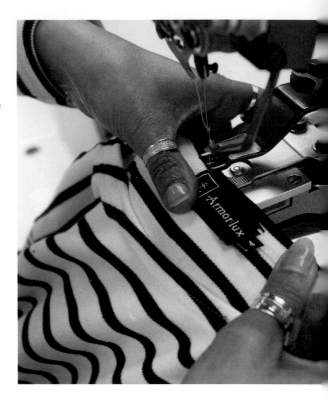

CONSTRUCTION OF KNITTED AND BONDED FABRICS

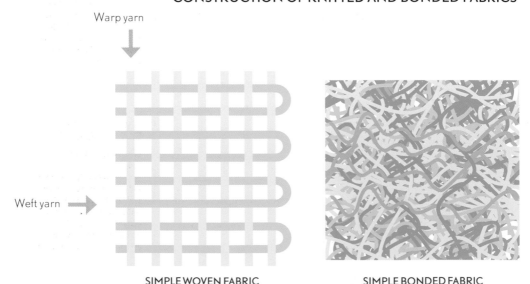

Warp yarn

Weft yarn

SIMPLE WOVEN FABRIC   SIMPLE BONDED FABRIC

Fabric types

There are two main types of fabric construction that are developed from knitting or weaving yarns, which are discussed in more detail below.

Knitted, woven, and bonded fabrics

Knitted fabrics are usually created by looping a single yarn or multiple yarns together. These looped yarns create horizontal and vertical connections, respectively called course and wale stitches. Woven fabrics are created when two yarns are interwoven together, with the warp yarn running down the length of a fabric and the weft yarn running across it.

Bonded fabrics are often used for linings, while garment interlinings are created by simply sticking fibers together. Fabrics can be dyed either at the yarn stage or even at the finished fabric or garment stage—a technique known as 'piece dyeing'. Sometimes, fabrics are held undyed in a 'greige' state—this allows buyers to make color dyeing decisions closer to the season.

No fashion buyer could ever hope to know about every type of fiber of yarn available; however, most have a good working knowledge of textiles science due to the various decisions that they have to make regarding the suitability of the fabric and yarn for the garments that they buy.

Printed fabrics

Prints come in every conceivable size, color, and genre, so it is hardly surprising that print trends are frequently one of the key determining factors when planning a fashion range. The size, construction, and repeat length of a print can have a dramatic impact on the cost of a garment. This is particularly true with large prints, as during the matching/ cutting processes, large areas of printed fabric may be wasted. Given the speed with which fashion trends travel, buyers often seek print exclusivity in order to give their range a competitive edge.

9

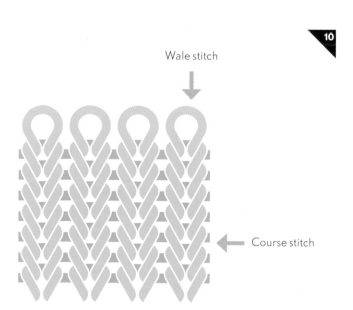

Wale stitch

Course stitch

SIMPLE WEFT KNITTED FABRIC

10

9   HAND VERSUS MACHINE

Fabrics, and how they handle during manufacturing, vary a great deal. That said, the human hand of the machinist cannot be replaced by either robots or machines.

10 THE THREE BASIC TYPES OF FABRIC

Buyers need to remain constantly aware of new yarn and fabric developments, which improve the material that they have to work with. Technological advances in textiles have created some innovative (and expensive) options for the fashion market.

Fabric lead times and the fashion buying cycle

In general, fabric manufacturers develop new fabrics, designs, prints and looks over a minimum period of twelve months ahead of the season in which they will be made into a range of garments. Therefore, unless a fashion buyer is working for an extremely large organization, it is normal for them to buy fabrics that have been already created for preexisting ranges. Occasionally, however, some large-scale buyers will involve themselves with the design of a fabric from scratch. Specific color and print decisions can normally be left to around six months ahead of the planned buying season.

Sourcing trips

Twice a year, private label buyers will undertake sourcing trips to both existing and potential new suppliers in key manufacturing areas. These trips generally extend over a two-week period, often with groups of buyers and management traveling together, but with the aim of visiting different suppliers.

These early visits are made for the development of samples, planning, and outlining production and delivery, as well as for seeking out new products, suppliers, and/or brands. At the same time, buyers will also try to visit interesting shopping areas in a foreign city in search of new and exciting products to bring into the fashion mix.

Foreign travel is seen by many as a perk of the job, although in reality, it is very demanding given the level of preplanning required and the intensity of the workload involved (buyers will often schedule up to six meetings per day). Increasingly, buyers from developed countries (where home-based manufacturing is on the decline) need to travel to global manufacturing markets such as those in India, Bangladesh, Turkey, and the Far East (especially China).

Often, suppliers from outlying factories will agree to meet buyers in centrally based buying offices in order to help buyers maximize their working time. On occasion, merchandisers will join these trips, mainly for the purpose of production planning.

11

11 SOURCING FABRICS

Many manufacturers will have predesigned and manufactured textiles available for buyers to select from, making lead times much faster.

THE FASHION GARMENT SUPPLY CHAIN

1 Fiber maker

2 Yarn manufacturer (dyeing)

3 Knitter/weaver (dyeing 2)
knitted or woven

ABROAD

4 Garment manufacturer

5 Shipping agent

6 Shipped by air/sea/road/rail
or a combination

**12 THE FASHION
GARMENT
SUPPLY CHAIN**

This diagram illustrates the
supply chain for both classic
retail sales and Internet sales,
showcasing the various hands
involved in the process from
manufacturer to consumer.

CLASSIC RETAIL FORMAT   INTERNET SALES

7 Arrives at retailer's distribution center

8 Distributed by road to fashion outlet

HOME

9 Arrives in retail store

10 Consumer

12

Fabric lead times and the fashion buying cycle

Fashion buyers and fabric sourcing

All buyers want to give their garments an edge over those of their competitors and sourcing innovative fabrics can play a key part in achieving this. As part of their everyday work, professional fashion buyers continually research and seek out new, exciting fabrics. More innovative fibers and yarns are constantly being developed to give each fabric manufacturer a competitive edge—but the speed with which such innovation arrives in the shops varies greatly.

Buyers at different market levels buy fabrics at prices that can be sensibly made into garments for their particular market level. The market prices of fabric vary dramatically from anywhere between a couple of dollars to more than $3,000 per square meter.

Always keep in mind that the square meterage of fabric used in garment construction varies dramatically by garment (compare, for instance, the material needed for a bikini to that required to create a bridal dress with a full train). Buyers need to quickly work out the square meterage required for their own product types, as well as the upper and lower limit prices that they can afford to pay per square meter.

PRODUCTION LEAD TIMES

All of these factors, either singly or in conjunction, affect lead times. The general drivers of production lead times are as follows:

×   The general economic situation in the consuming country. A good economy means high demand for garments and in turn heavily booked factories.
×   The complexity of the product being bought means demand on more specialist manufacturers. Factories producing complex knitted garments are often booked further ahead than those involved in making simple woven tops. This is because setting up complex knitting machines is much more difficult and capital-intensive than is the cutting and sewing required to produce simply designed woven cotton tops.
×   The availability and lead time of fabrics, linings, buttons, and trimmings.
×   The point in time: well before a season starts, factories are often quieter meaning short lead times. Once a season has started, repeat orders from the general market push out deliveries.
×   The timing of local holidays, especially the Chinese New Year—a lunar cycle festival during which time most factories close. Buyers need to be mindful of these dates as so much is bought from China.
×   How on trend a certain garment type or fabric is in a particular season can lead to high demand.
×   Currency movements—if the local currency appears cheap for buyers in the manufacturing country, this will lead to high demand.

13–14   CHANGING TECHNOLOGY

Weaving looms and knitting machines are now getting faster and are today able to weave and knit increasingly intricate designs and patterns. The savvy buyer will ensure that they always stay abreast of all new technological developments.

13
14

Fashion buyers need to regularly meet with all of the following people, departments, and/or organizations:

- × Sales persons/representatives/agents of large fabric manufacturers
- × Fabric merchants—who act as stockholders of bulk fabric (usually for smaller businesses)
- × In-house and external designers—who continually scan markets for new and unusual fabrics
- × Colleague buyers and garment in-house technologists—all of whom research regularly
- × Existing and potential manufacturers—who are all looking for the next new thing
- × Own cloth buyer/technologist—a few larger businesses do have a specialist function.

Selecting and buying garments

After fabric or yarn selection come the most important decisions—those concerning which garments are to go into the final range for eventual "sign off" by senior management. Normally, other than in very small businesses, the buyer will need to get their final range selection agreed by senior buying or board-level management before the final order is placed—or "signed off"—with the garment manufacturer.

In conjunction with the designer and their team merchandise planner, as well as working to a predetermined buying plan (stating the numbers of brands, styles, colors, and sizes that can be stocked in particular shops), the buyer will whittle down their initial wider sample selection into a final, narrower range. Many samples that were created during the previous six-month planning period will then be discarded, as buyers always sample more lines than can be included in a final range.

In Chapter 4, a greater understanding of the merchandise planning process will be introduced; and we will explore the importance of getting the right mix into retail shops, and how buyers and merchandisers work together to ensure the successful transition from manufacturer to retailer happens. This is a process that works prior to, during, and after the initial sourcing and communication between buyers and suppliers.

15 LADIESWEAR BUYERS

Ladieswear fashion buyers have a much wider range of garments available to buy than do their menswear counterparts simply because of the infinite flexibility of styles, types, and designs on offer.

15

16 MENSWEAR BUYERS

The male wardrobe has a more limited repertoire of garment types than that of women.

16

Case study: Primark

Primark, the successful discount retailer, has a remarkable story. The small retail operation that first started out of Dublin at the tail end of the 1960s has today turned into an empire throughout Western Europe, with stores successfully operating in Ireland, the Netherlands, Belgium, Germany, Austria, Portugal, Spain and, of course, the UK.

17

Originally founded as Penneys (not to be confused with USA retailer, J.C. Penney)—which it is still known as in Ireland—Primark is headquartered in Dublin and sells apparel, accessories, and home goods largely aimed at low-to-moderate income families. Primark strives to provide low-cost, high-fashion styles that capitalize on the fast fashion market.

Having a large market in Western Europe enables the company to purchase goods in bulk, providing considerable savings to the company that are then in turn passed directly on to the consumer. The feel-good factor provided to Primark's happy customers by cheap product means that the company can rely on consumers to provide the word-of-mouth advertising that is needed to keep generating sales; this also allows the company to redirect corporate monies elsewhere.

Primark is a business-savvy retailer with strong roots in the European market and is a rapidly expanding enterprise that smaller retailers can take great inspiration from.

17 FAST FASHION FORWARD
Primark is known for its inexpensive, fashion-forward looks that are born right off the runway. Buyers use extremely quick turnaround times to get fashion trends fast-tracked from runway to retail shop, sometimes in as little as six weeks.

Interview: Liam O'Farrell

Liam O'Farrell is Buying Controller for Primark.
A fashion and clothing man with a lifetime's
experience of buying and sourcing fashion products
from around the globe, Liam O'Farrell has spent
his career with the world-renowned Irish retailer
Penneys, now a subsidiary of the Primark group,
Europe's leading discount fashion retailer. O'Farrell
started with Penneys as a store management
trainee; moving up the store management ladder,
he was quickly promoted into a junior buying role.
Once in the buying office, his career lifted off and
he soon progressed, learning his skills as he moved
from garment area to garment area. He was a rising
star who was spotted by the legendary Arthur Ryan,
the founder and current CEO of the Primark empire.
Liam's skill and expertise soon saw him as the
buying controller for the Penneys/Primark group;
seeking out new supply sources during the meteoric
expansion of Primark. His knowledge of international
buying and sourcing is second to none.

Q Sourcing is a relatively new
specialist discipline in the
world of fashion buying.
Why do you think it has had
to come into being?

A As international fashion
retailers have become
larger, the volumes they
require have increased—
to find these large sources
required a different set of
skills to those of buying.
It has enabled buyers to
focus on developing
best-selling products,
while the sourcing managers
ensure that factories are
able to produce the
required volume at the
right quality level.

Q Fashion sourcing is a very different discipline from fashion buying: could you define the difference?

A The sourcing department is primarily there to find the source and then to hand over the new relationship to the buyer as soon as possible. The supplier/buyer relationship is the most sacrosanct relationship of all. Sourcing is about finding, and buying is about the subsequent nurture and development of the relationship.

Q During your career in international buying and sourcing, what things have changed the most?

A The geography of sourcing. When I started, it was all about Korea, Taiwan, Hong Kong, and the Philippines—who have now moved away from manufacturing to become administrative centers and/or producers of high-value fashion products. Latterly, Indonesia, China, India, Pakistan, and Bangladesh are the new players. Ethical issues are now massively important when selecting supply sources; nobody really cared—or indeed understood—about ethics when I first started.

Q What are the main criteria you use when seeking new sources of fashion production?

A First, the best suppliers in my mind are those who are good communicators and who therefore understand what you want quickly and efficiently. The cut and make-up are also critical— they must be able to make at the quality and price relevant to your business. As an aside, my view is that most factory issues are created by buyers not deciding on time or failing to give clear instructions.

Interview: Liam O'Farrell

Q Do you think that fashion buyers do a good job of sourcing or do you believe that they require the help of a specialist?

A Buyers tend to be very good at the short-term issues of sourcing; but in the long term company partnerships need to be handled separately.

Q What techniques or methods do you use for seeking out new sources of fashion supply?

A First, it's always important to check which countries competitors are buying from—it's often shown on their labels. Often, people involved in the trade are also knowledgeable.

Q Once you find and engage a new source of supply, what are the main issues and problems that you generally face?

A Getting a new supplier used to your own company's culture sometimes take a while. Also, they need to get to know what you want from them. Again, good communication is essential in the relationship. When dealing in huge quantities, you cannot afford to make assumptions.

Q How good do you believe most fashion retail businesses are at seeking out and developing new sources of supply?

A Often not very good, as they become used to the suppliers that they already have. For example, take a country like Bangladesh: the business there is developing so quickly, you have to keep visiting new factories to keep up with the situation. Many fashion retailers don't keep looking and searching.

Q Do you think that it is a good idea to change fashion suppliers as a matter of course—or are long-term business relationships better?

A Long-term relationships are important, but you should never stop searching for the next best. It's important to keep your ranges and looks fresh. If possible with long-term relationships, it's best that you request your key suppliers not to deal with your direct competitors—they will usually comply.

Q What are the essential personal requirements to be good at fashion sourcing?

A You need a good eye for your product; you must know your customer; you should understand the basics of finance; and finally you need to keep up-to-date with things that affect the business generally, like which countries are duty-free, for instance. You have to be certain that a particular supplier can actually make the goods that you want—they all need a good design base.

Q If you were asked to give new entrants into fashion buying and sourcing key advice, what would it be?

A You must stay curious and never stop searching; there are always new suppliers and countries coming on stream. Keep looking at competitors' labels and the trade press—you need to be a good detective.

"The supplier/buyer relationship is the most sacrosanct relationship of all. Sourcing is about finding, and buying is about the subsequent nurture and development of the relationship."

Chapter 3 summary

In this chapter, the buyer<>supplier relationship was introduced and we looked at the various players in the supply chain that support the selection and design of the final range. The buyer's research and communication strategies were discussed, and the need for buyers to be excellent time managers and forward thinkers was reiterated. Sourcing issues, such as lead times and sustainability, were touched on, highlighting the potential opportunities of working in a competitive global market. Range selection must-knows, such as textile science and product development, and more specifically the buyer's role within this process, were discussed to enable a greater understanding of the hard work and attention to detail that is needed for successful seasonal purchases.

Questions and discussion points

Having read about how product sourcing works to create the perfect offer for the customer, consider from your own shopper's perspective:

1. Which fashion shop that you regularly shop in provides the best overall product offer?

2. What aspect(s) of that shop's range(s) make this offer so good?

3. When you go shopping for your own clothes, what are the most important attributes of a fashion range that you most look for?

4. What sort of themes or displays in fashion store windows make you stop and look?

5. Consider whether the fashion shops that you frequent have too little or too much stock on the shop floor. What actually constitutes too little or too much stock?

6. Can you actually remember what was in the window the last time that you passed your favorite fashion shop—colors/themes/process/types of garment?

Exercises

As buyers undertake regular competitive shopping trips, they need to develop objective observational skills about the commerciality of competitors' ranges that will help them (and management) to develop the next season's range.

Working individually or as a group, visit two local fashion outlets (retailer A and retailer B). Select competitive fashion retailers targeting customers between the ages of 16–25. Answer the questions below as you browse around each outlet (you may need to make several visits). Write up notes outside and not as you examine the stock—retailers may be sensitive about researchers working openly in their stores, so don't make it too obvious.

1   In each of your outlets, select one department (e.g. dresses, blouses, jeans), then carefully go through the lines stocked and answer the following:

  ×   How many different individual styles are displayed on the shopfloor in your chosen department?
  ×   What size ranges are being stocked in both? Do they vary?
  ×   Do they have at least one size of every color available on the shopfloor? If not, try to estimate what percentage of size and color options are unavailable to customers.
  ×   How many different colors or prints are on offer in each department?

2.   Having visited the two outlets to have a detailed look at one product department in each, prepare a ten-minute verbal presentation aimed at a buying manager, then answer the following questions (comparing retailer A with retailer B's chosen product department):

  ×   Which has the wider product offer and by how much; for example, how many individual lines or styles are displayed?
  ×   Compare the size range stocked by each— comment on which has the widest size offer.
  ×   Compare both departments as to which has a greater depth of stock: which stocks the most units of any one individual size and colorway?
  ×   Which of the two departments has the most 'balanced' offer?

1

MERCHANDISE PLANNING

4

Many senior directors and managers enter the industry via the merchandising rather than the buying route, but few young entrants to the fashion business consider the merchandising pathway—yet it represents an interesting and rewarding job. In this chapter, we will examine the close relationship between the fashion buyer and the fashion merchandiser, and put the complex process of merchandise planning into context. Merchandising here relates to the numerical and logistical planning that brings product from manufacturer to retailer, which relies on meticulous advanced planning.

Solid fashion buying and merchandising practices are essential to maximize profitability, so fashion buyers in turn have their business performance measured using Key Performance Indicators (KPI), which are driven by the business's overall financial objectives. Hitting the sales and stock plan is therefore crucial for all fashion businesses.

1   SPRING/SUMMER 2010

For this season's collection, Balmain prêt-à-porter womenswear showcased the label's trademark rock-chick sexiness, embellished with intensely worked embroidery.

What is merchandise planning?

Merchandise planners have to gauge daily, weekly, and seasonal demand for what is probably one of the most difficult consumer products to predict. This difficulty arises from a number of factors, of which the need to successfully monitor and control stock is perhaps the most significant. If a fashion business has too little stock, it will potentially lose sales to competitors; on the other hand, if it has too much stock, it will have invested buying money that is effectively 'dead'.

More problematically, this 'dead' stock will clutter up the retail environment, preventing retailers from displaying other successful merchandise, which in turn makes the shop floor uninteresting to consumers. This scenario ultimately leads to lower profitability as a result of fewer sales and heavy end-of-season price reductions (markdowns), RTVs (return to vendor) or charitable donations.

Other than a few basic garments, such as plain hosiery, simple underwear, or workwear, there are very few items of merchandise that can be successfully carried over from one season to another. This is why there is a strong need for solid merchandise planning within the retail organization. These planners work with buyers and other organization members to ensure that the right product is allocated to shops on a timely basis. Planners also help to transition seasonal product as well as to aid in the logistical distribution of goods between other shop locations (if there are any).

Fashion buying is one of the most complex consumer products to buy, for the following reasons:

Unpredictability
Fashions and trends change rapidly and frequently—this can leave businesses with excess unsellable stock that reduces overall profitability.

Seasonality
Seasons require different types and weights of fabric and clothing type—weather is extremely unpredictable, with rapid changes of product demand. Getting the right level of supply is therefore always a problem.

Product complexity
There are so many different types of garments available to men, women and children. Outerwear, underwear, formal, and casual clothing, combined with size and color options, create literally thousands of individual stock-keeping units (SKUs).

2 KPIs

Reviewing key performance indicators (KPIs) allows both buyers and merchandisers to quickly and aggressively react to business that may lead to less profit if otherwise left alone (discussed in further detail later in the chapter).

The buyer< >merchandiser relationship

In relation to fashion buying, merchandising management is often confused as being related to another fashion skill – namely, visual merchandising. Yet, merchandising related to buying is very different and requires high levels of numeracy in order to successfully regulate the planning, monitoring, and controlling of the buyer's proposed purchases.

Visual merchandising, on the other hand, is where an individual works to create a conducive environment that will entice consumers to purchase goods through strategic product placement and visual displays. Sometimes, the job description of a retail visual merchandiser may include that of merchandiser if the retailer is small enough.

Working together, the buyer and merchandiser typically hold similar levels of managerial authority. They usually work very closely together to ensure that their buying team (usually a one product department) achieves their specific Key Performance Indicators (KPIs)—a set of well-defined financial objectives required of each buying department for that season.

When new ranges are being planned, or during regular reviews of trading performance, the buyer and merchandiser nearly always meet management together. When a buyer is ill or travelling, a good merchandiser can even make minor day-to-day buying decisions alone. Similarly, good buyers are extremely numerate and are able to make minor planning and operational decisions related to the merchandising role.

At the start of a new season, the buyers and merchandiser are effectively controlling and buying three seasons of stock:

× **Last season**—clearing and marking-down slow lines
× **Current season**—delivering, monitoring, and reacting to sales by buying more or less product
× **Future season**—planning samples, writing orders, and planning delivery phasing.

The need for buyers and merchandisers to be very disciplined, organized, and responsive is obvious from the complexity of this task, not least because they will eventually be measured on their performance by the KPIs, as laid down by upper management.

KEY PERFORMANCE INDICATORS

2

SUPPLY ON HAND/ DAYS OF SUPPLY

HOW LONG IT WILL TAKE A SHOP TO SELL THROUGH ITS CURRENT INVENTORY OF A PARTICULAR ITEM—TYPICALLY DENOTED IN WEEKS OR MONTHS

STOCK TO SALES RATIO

THE NUMBER OF ITEMS YOU CURRENTLY HAVE ON HAND VS. THOSE YOU HAVE SOLD— SHOWN AS A PERCENTAGE (INVERSELY RELATED TO SELL-THROUGH PERCENTAGE)

GMROI

GROSS MARGIN RETURN ON INVESTMENT. HOW MUCH YOU MADE VS. HOW MUCH YOU INVESTED. THIS IS CALCULATED BY TAKING TOTAL DOLLAR INVESTED MINUS TOTAL DOLLAR MADE ON A PARTICULAR PRODUCT

What is merchandise planning?

The buyers instinct vs. planning

Historically, buyers had more direct authority over actually purchasing product, especially in the days when the big store buyers had little numerical planning support or computerized stock control systems—all of which are now widely available at every level of the trade.

However, global fashion markets are becoming tougher, more changeable and faster-moving—and competition is becoming ever more intense. In addition, consumers are becoming more demanding than ever, wanting ceaselessly fast turnaround. Consumers are also continually breaking down into smaller market segments, further challenging retailers.

Consumers are now able to buy through a multitude of channels to immediately get what they want, whether this being the Internet, a mail order catalog or a high-street shop. They are becoming increasingly influential in the fashion buying process too, mainly as a result of personal communication technologies and the faster transmission of ideas (i.e. social media and smartphones).

3 CHANGING MARKETS

With the continual introduction of consumer micro-markets, buyers must not only use strategic planning but also need to develop an instinct for the business to aid in the selection of the final product range.

"What you wear is how you present yourself to the world, especially today, when human contact is so quick. Fashion is instant language."

Miuccia Prada

Doing things the old way by trying to plan everything six to nine months ahead is no longer realistic. Buyers, and particularly merchandisers, now have to react faster to changes in consumer demand—that is, with a fast fashion response. Obviously, buyers and merchandisers still have to plan well ahead to ensure delivery from foreign factories, but they also have to be able to quickly switch plans and generate fast responses to changing consumer demands.

There is no doubt that a far more complex fashion buying world lies ahead for all of us than that which has gone before. Buyers are now required to meet higher standards than ever before and today, thanks to technology, their performance can also be directly tracked to KPIs.

3

What is merchandise planning?

How a buyer's success is judged

Buyers are generally well paid as it is their professionalism, skill, and ability that picks out next season's winning lines. Picking winners has often been called "having an eye," but many young entrants fail to realize just how financially driven fashion buyers also need to be. Fun in fashion requires firm finances first and foremost.

As mentioned earlier in this chapter, each product buying team will have agreed with management to a series of KPIs against which that team will be monitored and judged. If all buying teams achieve their planned KPIs, then the business will make good profit and so thrive and survive. Most buying teams receive bonuses on top of their basic salary, assuming that they achieve a majority (or sometimes all) of their planned KPIs.

At the start of buying for a new season, a basic sales plan is agreed as the first step, usually followed by a profit plan. Profit can loosely be described as the difference between the cost price from the factory and the price at which a garment is sold in a shop.

In general, last year's (LY) trading performance forms the basis against which a buying plan is created. If a department has traded well, it is described as "on trend" and similarly for "off trend" performances. In fashion, it unlikely that all departments are on trend at once—sometimes, dresses become a must-have item for a few seasons only to be seen as old-fashioned a mere season later. Garments, like individual fashions themselves, wax and wane in the fashion stakes.

4

KPI descriptors

Some of the normal KPIs used in fashion buying offices are described below. There are other KPIs, but these are the most important ones required for overall fashion planning, control, and monitoring purposes:

Planned sales

× actual money taken at retail in local currency
× daily/weekly/monthly/seasonally/ annually.

Last Year (LY) sales

× actual money taken at retail in local currency in same period for the previous year
× daily/weekly/monthly/seasonally/ annually.

Forecast sales

× merchandisers' best estimate of sales going forward +/– plan
× daily/weekly/monthly/seasonally/ annually.

Stock level

× a valuation of stock in the business, expressed at retail value in local currency
× end of day/week/season or year.

Gross Margin (GM)

× the difference between what the buyer pays and what all the stock is sold at, expressed as a total cash value and as a percentage.

Stock Turn/Weeks Cover (ST/WC)

This is an efficiency ratio. Good fashion businesses turn their stock over quickly; this is called high stock turn. This week's cover refers to the number of weeks that your stock would last until it sold out. The fewer weeks of stock = the faster the Stock Turn (ST) = efficient buying and selling = higher profit.

Markdown Level

Even the best fashion businesses have some slow lines that require price reductions to sell out. The fewer lines reduced the better: an indicator that the buyer is buying good stock. Although it may seem unfeasible, it is good practice for businesses to plan markdown each season.

Markdown is expressed as a cash valuation (sometimes as a percentage) of the number of items marked down multiplied by how much they are reduced by. Occasionally, prices are marked up, for example as manufacturing costs go up or currency exchange rates fluctuate.

Net Achieved Margin After Discount (NAMAD)

This is the difference between the gross margin less the profit lost as a result of having to mark poor-selling stock down— sometimes known as the "net buying margin." This is the best indicator of a buyer's level of overall profitable buying success.

Gross margin (GM) – profit lost (a negative loss) = NAMAD.

4 ASSORTED MARKDOWNS

When retail shops put out massive clearance racks, this could be a strong indicator that the buying team bought too much of a multiple assortment or that a given trend ended before stock could be depleted.

What is merchandise planning?

The merchandise planning process

All fashion businesses begin planning at "top level" in order to estimate how much merchandise they plan to sell (hence buy) ahead of the season. The two main trading seasons are autumn/winter (early September–February) and spring/summer (March–August). After initial negotiations with management, buyers will be given the future season's retail sales plan (or budget) to buy with—typically around six months ahead of the start of the season.

The merchandiser will then work closely with the buyer over the course of a series of regularly scheduled planning meetings to break the overall retail sales plan down. This is necessary to determine how many ranges, lines, sizes, and colors will be needed to deliver a cohesive and logical range to the shop chain. The process is complex and mainly draws upon historical sales data, combined with the buyer's views, future assumptions, and trend information.

Buyers will typically use the detailed range plan to buy against. Working with suppliers, the buyer will specify the amount needed for delivery into the business by line, by week, and by color. However, some more edgy and directional businesses do plan less tightly, purposefully leaving the buyer with a buying allowance, called "Open to Buy" (OTB), that is bought just before the due delivery date, depending on the latest fashion trend or demand.

Planning all of a range too far in advance in any fashion business can be dangerous—hence the need to leave OTB flexibility. Such range plans are usually written in a spreadsheet format, which in turn are part of a larger and more complex merchandise planning and control system, which helps to control, monitor, and manage the entire supply chain from manufacturer through to shop.

5

Approximately 15 months ahead of the commencement of the selling season, buyers and merchandisers will generally discuss a top-down sales plan which senior management will propose and discuss with the individual product buying and merchandising teams during initial planning. At this stage, the buyer and merchandiser will work together with management to decide on the overall level of buying needed to achieve the proposed planned sales.

All initial planning is based on overall retail selling value, and it is for the buyer and merchandiser to go away and decide precisely what percentage of each product categories could (if agreed) go to make up this plan. Senior management will then await the team's first look at how the buying money will be split up.

The buyer takes the lead in deciding which product types are likely to be on or off trend in the future season being planned. This is where the buyer's intuition and the merchandiser's historical knowledge and experience converge in producing the first outline of the buying plan. During the six months before buying actually commences, (probably for the season that lies 12 months ahead), this basic plan will gradually become more detailed and cohesive.

PRODUCT ASSORTMENT PLANNING

This describes the process of determining exactly what quantities (and attributes) of each product classification a buyer will need to purchase based on the following factors:

Brands
Are you buying private labels or national brands? If so, what is the ratio of private labels to national brands? Which national brands will you add to the proposed range?

Size
Based on your consumer market and target audience, which sizes will you order? Will you have extended sizes offered online?

Color
Consumer color choices vary drastically, so keeping a varied assortment of both classic colors and seasonal trends is important. However, a buyer needs to determine the quantity of each color to order to maintain consistent stock levels.

Textile
Choosing the right fabrics for the season is imperative (as discussed in Chapter 3). A buyer will look at trends as well as market climates to make these decisions.

Buyers should be aware of previous seasons' sales, upcoming trends, and most importantly, consumer needs when initiating the planning process.

5 PLANNING MEETINGS

Buyers and merchandisers will meet regularly to discuss the upcoming range details, often including senior management in the meetings to ensure that sales forecasts and previous season's totals are accurate.

◀ What is merchandise planning?　　　　　Product sampling and final range preparation ▶

116

Developing the initial seasonal buying plan

An initial buying plan provides the first breakdown of how the budget is about to be spent by category. Category descriptors vary by individual business, but are generally self-explanatory. This initial breakdown into percentage of spend by category normally undergoes minor amendments as a result of problems, issues, events, and experiences until the "buying point" is reached. A multitude of factors can change initial category plans, such as changing fashion, fabric, or garment trends, for example. Fashion buyers want to be as confident as possible when buying; the closer to the season they are, the more likely they are to be right.

Forecasting sales and stock

Fashion buyers will work with all members of the retail organization, gathering information on previous season's sales, new shop openings, consumer preferences, etc. This information allows them to best gauge how and what to purchase for the next season's range.

While each retailer has their own in-house generated sales reports, many are similar in how they set about providing information on specific departments' sales from the previous year and/or season. This can be as detailed as providing specifics on color or size, or as broad as totaling sales for the entire class of womenswear.

These reports enable a buyer to forecast how each department will fare based on senior management provided totals, at which time they are able to make the appropriate buys necessary to achieve these specific sales goals. As the buyer and merchandiser work to plan the seasonal range, these planning proposals will become more detailed and precise, allowing all members of the organization to see the intended buying direction.

6　WOMENSWEAR
　　PLANNING MATRIX

Shown here is a broad flow of the planning and buying process from initial plan to the start of the season. Note that due to the differing lead times of product types and levels of fast fashion product involved with individual fashion businesses, this diagram represents an approximation only.

Product assortment varies based on numerous factors including season, regional location, current and/or future trends, and customer preferences.

TYPICAL FIRST PLANNING PROPOSAL – WOMENSWEAR SPRING/SUMMER

Department	Actual sales $K Last year [LY] (Spring/Summer)	Planned sales $K This year [TY] (Spring/Summer)	% +/– TY vs. LY	Rationale for + or – growth
Dresses	150	200	+33.3%	Trend forecaster sees strong 50s style revival
Blouses	100	110	+10%	Formal shirts not very "in"—move to casual look
Casual tops	200	250	+25%	Strong casual/easy fit look
Trousers	50	50	(or flat to LY)	Formal trousers not strong at shows
Shirts	100	150	+50%	Miniskirt making a comeback
Jeans	150	200	+33.3%	Massive interest in branded jeans and washes forecast
Shorts	25	50	+100%	Shorts extremely strongly forecast
Swimwear	80	100	+25%	Hot summer forecast = exciting new prints
Lingerie / Underwear	100	105	+5%	Steady/static—no new product
Hosiery	40	35	-12.5%	In decline—leg tanning more dominant trend
Accessories	80	100	+25%	Italian style handbags and sunglasses ever-popular
Grand total	$1075K	$1350K	+25.6% *	*denotes very strong overall planned growth for womenswear

6

◀ What is merchandise planning?　　　　　　Product sampling and final range preparation ▶

118

Developing the initial seasonal buying plan

Merchandise assortments

After reviewing sales reports to help create the seasonal buying range, buyers will look at the total assortment of goods, or the merchandise classification, to determine product-specific needs that the company may need to invest in for the season. For example, going into the spring season from winter, buyers will begin to dramatically scale back on heavy outerwear, coats and so on in order to make way for lighter-weight tops and bottoms in preparation for changing climate conditions.

A buyer may also be introduced to new silhouettes or materials from the manufacturer, at which time they will have to decide what this merchandise should be classified as (i.e. knits, wovens, casualwear, or eveningwear, etc.). Sometimes, product assortment is determined by climate, location, trend, or a combination of these factors.

Selecting and grading the store ranges

The key drivers to when and how a range is bought depend upon whether the buyer is buying national or private label goods. Buying a national or branded label is normally done much closer to the start of the season as the product design and factory negotiation processes have already been carried out by the brand; the buyer simply sub-selects from a range previously prepared for them.

Private label buying is much more complex, with a longer lead time than for branded buying. However, with both methods, it is still ultimately the buyer (in conjunction with the merchandiser) who has to reduce the range down to one that is right for a given business and based on the negotiated time frame.

7

Buyers will always have more samples than they can possibly fit into their final range selection, as stores always have size limitations. Individual shops in a chain all have varying floor areas, thus limiting sales floor and backstock space. Usually, businesses put similar-sized stores together into between five to ten store groupings. Each buying and merchandising team will plan the exact number of lines that will go to all stores, with the widest or most complete range of lines going to the very large stores.

Merchandisers and buyers spend a great deal of time grading ranges in order of importance. Deciding on ranges for smaller shops is in fact the hardest job, as this small range will have to satisfy the majority of customers with a limited offer—a very difficult thing to achieve.

7–8 SAMPLE REVIEW
A buyer will ensure garment samples match product specifications outlined during the initial sample order. Merchandisers work with the buyer to ensure that the product assortment allocated for each store is based on customer need, trends, location, etc.

8

Product sampling and final range preparation

Gathering and refining samples and/or fabric and color swatches is a continuous process during the range development process. Good buyers continually collect fabric ideas for color, texture, and design inspiration, which can then be used when developing private label ranges. Most buyers keep working files of cuttings, pictures, drawings, and photographs that they feel may be useful, in a similar way to fashion designers. Samples are then presented at the final range meeting, usually using live models to show the product to its best advantage.

Preparation for the final range

Although management will have been involved during the preceding months, reviewing line and range developments during regular planning meetings, it is the final range meeting that is the most important. It is here that the whole buying team will be expected to support the buyer's range, both in terms of design, buying quantities and the detailed category, color, size, and brand balance. Whether buying private label or selecting from a new branded range, all decisions are then generally ratified by management at the final preseason range presentation.

The sampling sequence for private label products

The sampling process for own-label products varies slightly according to individual buying offices, but generally has three distinct stages:

1. **The fit sample.** Often not actually manufactured in the final fabric, but it helps to develop and check the initial fit. Garments are usually made in a size 12 or medium and are tried out on the office's fit model. Any necessary alterations are then sent to the manufacturer to correct—the sample may go back and forth to the supplier a few times until a perfect fit is achieved.

2. **The final approval preproduction sample.** The final garment in the right color and fabric is delivered in all sizes, all of which are checked against the originally agreed fit sample. Fabric will have already been sent away for testing prior to this, to check color fastness, washing and dry cleaning performance, light fastness, wear durability, and other product-specific tests, such as chlorine resistance for swimwear.

3. **Production sample.** As manufacturing starts, early production samples are usually express air-freighted to the buyer and checked against the final approval sample. Things like labels, swing tickets, and care instructions are also checked.

"The bitterness of poor quality is remembered long after the sweetness of low price has faded from memory."
Aldo Gucci

Branded approach to sampling

When buying from national brands or designer ranges, suppliers' samples are often in short supply and the branded buyer is often unable to retain samples. In this case, images of samples will be provided by the supplier or will be taken by the buying team to later remind them of the range. For final branded range presentations, the garments' ranges are borrowed for the day and later returned.

Managing samples

All samples, whether for private label or branded buying purposes, are valuable items. They cost a great deal to make and are often unique: it is therefore vital that they do not get lost. The care, labelling, tracking, and movement of samples is a major responsibility of the buying assistants. Sample rails and sample rooms need to be constantly tidied and rearranged, ensuring that samples can be quickly located.

Sealing samples

Most buying operations "seal" samples—this means placing a metal or plastic non-removable seal attached by a wire loop on to samples once they have been checked and accepted. The buying office will seal at least two samples (sometimes more), sending one back to the manufacturer and retaining one or more for themselves.

Sealing samples ensures that if any product, quality, sizing, technical, or other disputes arise, then both parties can refer back to these agreed samples to check what was ordered. Sealing at all three stages is undertaken by larger fashion buying offices, often designating each stage with a different color code for each type of seal, to enable easier garment identification. With so many different types of samples moving in and out of fashion buying offices, the benefits of good sample management are obvious.

Promotional samples

As well as the flow of samples back and forth from buyer to suppliers, buying teams also have to contend with a fast and varied demand to loan samples out for other business-related purposes. These include:

× Internal and external press and fashion shows and events
× Photo shoots for shopping catalogs and visual merchandising purposes
× Photo shoots for advertising and PR
× Photographs for Internet shopping pages.

The level and type of sample demand made upon individual buyers and their buying teams obviously depends on the type and size of the fashion business involved.

Product sampling and final range preparation

The final range presentation meeting is necessary for buyers to get total "buy in" and agreement from the managers that the range represents the best selection of product for the targeted customer. This key meeting will probably also be attended by the in-house design team and the QA team. Other attendees at a final range meeting might include the directors and/or heads of buying and merchandising. Often, the head of a company might also be present.

Presenting the final range

Presenting the final range can therefore be a very stressful time for both buyer and merchandiser who will aim to "work" the meeting together to confirm the rationale and logic of their range proposals. It is at times like these that a buyer's verbal communication skills are tested to the full, so both buyer and merchandiser need to be well prepared as they finally present the culmination of many months of planning work.

The merchandiser will have prepared highly detailed, numerically based planning sheets that clearly show the sizes, colors, delivery dates, store grades, and anticipated profit margins, as well as the percentage of the OTB (open to buy) that is to be spent on other product categories.

The size and proposed growth of each category in comparison to that achieved in the previous year will be examined, with the buyer justifying their products and range to all assembled. Often, a fit model will be used to show off key garments to their fullest advantage; other garments may be hung up on wall rails or grids, with smaller items pinned on to display boards.

Good buying and merchandising teams will probably have only minor alterations and suggestions made to them by management at the end of the presentation. These will be recorded and action-checked to ensure later follow-up by the buying and merchandising teams. If a buying team has previously had a difficult trading season, it is usual for management to spend more time ensuring that these past problems are not repeated again.

Both the fashion buyer and merchandiser need to be confident in the final range presentation meeting in order to succeed. Uncertainty, lack of conviction, poorly researched facts, and weak rationale are no basis for company directors to sign off on the intended range.

9 SPRING/SUMMER 2010

Presentation of the final collection of Philip Lim's prêt-à-porter womenswear on the runway, designed to show off key garments to their fullest advantage. Department heads and buying/merchandising teams look for risk and range issues within the final presentation.

9

Risk and range size issues

Although more unusual colors, prints, and styles may have been trend forecasted as the season's newest 'in' look, the reality is that the majority of fashion customers err on the cautious side, not wanting to stand out from the crowd. Good fashion buyers and merchandisers realize that their range needs these fashion elements, but tend to under-buy the extremes of fashion which, if left over at the end of the season, will require price reductions to clear stock levels which may damage overall profitability.

Reducing levels of riskier merchandise

The fashion press and associated marketeers love to feature the more leading and extreme fashion styles—although seasoned buyers buy into extremes more cautiously. However, even the most conservative fashion buyers buy enough of the riskier fashion pieces, in order to ensure that their department balance gives the right overall first impression to consumers.

The idea of selling short (that is, deliberately running out before the end of a season) of riskier merchandise makes good commercial sense, although this is sometimes hard to explain to the uninitiated. It is always better to have too much black left (as this is a classic color that never goes out of fashion and will continue selling through the next season), than a neon fluorescent color with limited seasonal carry-over potential.

Getting the size balance right

Although there are international clothing size standards, there is a great deal of garment size variation between different retailers and brands, all selling what is labeled as the same size.

Some retailers use 'vanity sizing' whereby the size shown on the garment is actually one size smaller than the product's physical dimensions. This is intended to flatter the customer, who is then more inclined to buy as a result of believing that they are smaller than they actually are. This is really sharp practice, but most customers are not easily fooled and could come to distrust the brand.

What customers most want from a range is for their size to be available and for a garment to fit well. Customers who can rely on a brand, shop or range's consistency of fit will usually come back. Getting fit right and having sizes always available is a strong customer draw. This is especially so for jeans, shoes, intimates, and tailoring, where close body fit is an imperative. Good fashion buyers spend a great deal of time on getting fit right. Merchandisers spend even more time ensuring size availability.

Range width and depth

Differently sized and different types of fashion retail outlet can offer dramatically different numbers of product lines. Smarter upmarket shops tend to spread their stock out, enabling customers to focus more easily on the design and quality of the product. In very expensive and more upmarket retail outlets, the old adage of "less is more" is clearly evident. In discount shops, the opposite is generally true, with bulging, overfilled rails and shelves—making customer choice often difficult and confusing.

10 JUDGING RANGE DEPTH

No fashion retailer can ever offer 100% color, size or line availability—this is another key issue faced by buyers and merchandisers.

Buyers work endlessly with merchandisers and store space planners to get the right number of lines allocated for each different size or group of shop(s). In large department stores, thousands of individual fashion lines are stocked, whereas a small boutique might only carry a few hundred. Retail space is the main driver of range offer or range width within any individual retail organization.

Another key issue faced by buyers and merchandisers is how much stock of each individual line to carry in store, especially of each size and color. Stocking all sizes and colors all of the time is a fashion ideal, but is rarely the case. Fringe large and small sizes are only carried in small quantities, because the statistical demand odds for them are generally lower than for the median consumer sizes. Very small quantities of a fringe size/color are typically stocked in store, which will be immediately replenished during the next shipment delivery date (or as soon as possible).

No fashion retailer can ever offer 100 percent color, size or line availability—although many set availabilities of 90 percent as a key performance criteria. To overcome this out-of-stock problem, customers are sometimes offered a next-day home or store delivery—thus avoiding a lost sale. This is sometimes referred to as a 'walk-away'. Other options might include retailers offering to order the item via the company's website, or having the shop contact another location with the aim of securing the requested item.

Getting the range balance right

A key skill of any buyer is to ensure that when customers walk into one of their retail outlets, the range immediately excites them and makes them want to browse, stop, try on and hopefully... purchase something! Subconsciously, we all make a quick judgment as we walk past a shop window or walk through a department. Getting the range balance right is the secret to creating this instant appeal; and again, is a skill that is highly developed in the best and most successful fashion buyers.

Good range balance means getting the following things right:

× Good overall first impression upon entry suitable for the targeted customer's chosen ranges
× Clearly visible, relevant, and fashionable color, design, and/or style offer
× Good relevant selection of brands —especially important for branded merchandise retailers
× Good value and clear pricing (not necessarily the cheapest)
× Stock availability in all sizes, colors, designs, and fits—often the hardest goal to achieve.

If the merchandise planning process has been carried out by the buyer and merchandiser in advance then a good range balance will generally follow. In turn, getting the range right will be rewarded by achieving the planned level of sales and hopefully more.

11 SPRING/SUMMER 2010

Elie Saab's haute couture collection featured diaphanous evening dresses as part of a perfectly balanced range designed to seduce both buyers and consumers.

11

Today's consumers are used to instant gratification, in terms of locating and buying fashion products immediately. They also expect endless choice. Fashion buyers and merchandisers know that if you fail to attract immediately and to provide the exact product by size and color, most customers will simply walk away to your competitors (or try to find what they want on the Internet).

Stock held off the floor in stockrooms has no chance of selling at all. To overcome this issue, retailers are working on developing very fast stock-replenishment systems, which replace sold-out stock almost immediately from the central distribution center.

While not directly involved in stock replenishment, buyers are aware of this problem so often plan lines that might easily become satisfactory replacements for the customer if their first choice is not available. Fashion buyers work tirelessly to review option availability with their merchandisers and senior buying management. Perfection is never possible, but buying a well-balanced range overall can greatly assist in switching consumers to another similar best-selling line in the range.

Everything about buying a fashion range is a question of balance. In the next chapter, we will look at new trends in the buying industry that ultimately enable buyers to remain one step ahead of the retail game.

Case study: SAP

Every retail organization has to have a strong logistics system in place to manage the flow of information and/or artifacts going from one place to another. SAP is a company built from the ground up to offer software solutions that help retailers (and a plethora of other industries) to put these systems into place.

12

Headquartered in Walldorf, Germany, with over 125 offices in the global arena, SAP has been a significant market leader in enterprise application software for the past 40 years. SAP is best known for its work in mobile solutions, applications, and analytics, but have recently started to move into developing cloud solutions and databases.

Retailers frequently turn to this software giant to help gauge business performance; and specifically, to gain further information about the sales and profitability of divisions, classes, SKUs, and so on for the buying range—past, present, and future

12 TECHNOLOGY AT WORK

SAP gets the chance to show off new software that can be used in mobile P.O.S. systems during a technology conference. Continually developing systems such as these make the buyer's job easier in relation to company logistics.

Interview: Stephen Henley

Stephen Henley currently works as European Retail Regional Industry Principal for Merchandise Planning/Assortment, Promotion and Pricing Solutions at SAP—one of the world's largest providers of software used by fashion buyers and merchandisers to analyze, plan, and control their ranges. Prior to joining SAP, Stephen worked for a variety of fashion companies, including Levi's, Timberland, House of Fraser, Debenhams, Dolcis, and Bertie.

At SAP, Stephen works with many of the world's leading fashion retailers and consumer goods companies to understand their requirements and assist in the design and delivery of planning and buying solutions that deliver true business benefits.

Stephen has a wealth of experience advising retailers in the UK, across Europe, and around the world on the information needs and systems that support successful fashion buying. During his career, he has seen seismic shifts in the way that businesses plan from a highly predetermined standpoint, to today's fast fashion retail that demands agile and flexible planning windows.

Q What is actually meant by the Buying Decision Support System (BDSS)?

A It is a software solution that helps you to analyze the performance of your business now and allows you to plan a road map of anticipated future performance of the ranges and styles that you propose to buy in the future.

Q Has the speed at which fashion ranges change impacted upon the way BDSS applications have developed and how they are now being used in fashion buying?

A Yes, they have changed greatly. Historically, fashion buyers and merchandisers tended to look backwards to determine the future. With the emergence of fast fashion, "looking in the rear view mirror" is now less and less relevant as a guide to future performance.

Both systems and people have to react in the moment; BDSS and those using it now have to react extremely quickly, before a style, look or brand goes off the boil.

With focused analytics, you have the ability to replan at the speed of the consumer allowing retail winners to stand out and differentiate themselves from the losers.

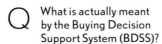

Q Is planning for fashion buying harder than for buying other consumer goods?

A Yes. Fashion has an extremely wide range of brands, products, sizes, and colors, which by their nature have very short and changeable product life cycles.

Now there are fewer continuity (or basic) lines and it is typical for fashion retailers to introduce monthly or bi-monthly collections or ranges spread over the classic spring/ summer and autumn/ winter seasons.

This means many more planning cycles and buying decisions have to be made and as a result, management are demanding greater flexibility, accuracy, planning control, and sourcing rigour from their buyers.

Q How does the SAP BDSS specifically help a fashion buyer with their work?

A Buying decisions are made in many different ways. For example, more and more consumers look on their smartphone for inspiration and then buy immediately online or collect from a nearby store. The buyer cannot possibly know how the consumer will interact with the brand or what they will buy very far in advance.

With fragmented and unpredictable consumer behavior, fashion buyers are less able to rely on history to anticipate demand or the strength of trends. Buyers now have to act and buy faster based on current customer demand, which also includes social media feedback and chatter trends. Sites like ASOS and ModCloth now talk with and ask their customers what they want and how they want it. This is a complete sea change from the past.

SAP's approach is to deliver systems that increasingly allow real-time consumer feedback to be embedded into the buyer's decision-making processes. We place customer-centricity at the center of all our BDSS innovation.

Interview: Stephen Henley

Q **So how exactly has this new consumer immediacy impacted a fashion buyer's planning process?**

A Increasingly, buyers will have to anticipate which customer groups are going to buy what products and from where. In the future, buyers will also need to ensure that the ranges stocked by the stores are clearly targeted to meet local or loyal customer preferences, as well as to support click-and-collect sales.

Buyers will be tasked with developing ranges for groups or 'tribes' that form the core of the retailers' loyal customer base. Targeted and localized ranges will become the norm based on customer preferences and buying behavior.

Q **Although fashion planning and buying is becoming more complex and difficult to anticipate, do fashion buyers still begin to plan using an overall seasonal sales plan?**

A Yes. It is still the case that buying teams are given an overall sales and profitability target for the classic spring/summer or autumn/winter season. This is referred to as "top down planning."

From this starting point, buyers break down the sales and profitability into product categories and at the same time plan how much of the overall sales number is likely to be sold through each channel; for example, how much via the web shop and how much in each shop. Hours are spent in buying offices planning, reviewing, and finally agreeing these numbers, as developing these plans is vital to the success of the business.

Q BDSS systems appear at first glance to be very complex. Do fashion buyers need to fully understand how they work, or is this more important for the merchandiser?

A Yes. Fashion buyers need to have a good grasp of the information and messages regarding sales trends that these systems deliver. They have to learn how to interrogate the systems to react quickly to customers' changing micro-demands. BDSS systems are becoming smarter and easier to use.

In addition, you will hear the terms "Google smart" and "Apple friendly" being used to describe how retail software suppliers are reengineering their user interfaces in response to the demands of a mobile-empowered buying community for clear visibility of trading and social media data.

Q Fashion customers vary greatly in every geographic location and the way in which they buy product(s). Can SAP's BDSS help the buyer to understand and respond to these varying demands?

A Yes. Our systems allow buyers and merchandisers to plan and buy their ranges in a customer-centric way. As customer demand patterns become more fragmented, it is vital to get the right mix of product bought and placed in the correct retail outlets, balanced with the more unusual demand patterns (for example, people in some geographical regions are shorter than in others).

We are able to plan micro-demands into our buying and allocation systems: BDSS systems can identify local trends and style preferences that include local customer nuances and that support the buyer in developing the right product range per store.

"With focused analytics, you have the ability to replan at the speed of the consumer allowing retail winners to stand out and differentiate themselves from the losers."

Interview: Stephen Henley

Q During your career, how have BDSS systems improved to the benefit of the fashion buyer?

A During my career, systems have continuously evolved to give buyers an understanding of what is happening. For most of this period, the evolution has focused on consolidating the huge data volumes to deliver the results in preconfigured reports.

The key focus of BDSSs in this period has been to provide comprehensive stock and sales reports as quickly as possible after the close of the trading period with limited exception management. In recent years, preconfigured analytics have been added to the systems and these have enabled buyers to more clearly identify trends, winning or failing styles.

There is no doubt that the changes in technology during my career mean that buyers make better decisions and are better informed than when I started. These changes have contributed to the national and international success of many famous UK fashion retail brands. However, I believe that we are still in the cusp of a revolution in retail BDSS solutions.

Q Where do you see BDSSs heading in terms of supporting fashion buying?

A There is no doubt in my mind that we are at the beginning of a revolution that will see radical change to the traditional BDSS enablers. Historically, buyers and merchandisers have used the BDSS module to take centralized chain-wide "command and control" decisions on trends, price, ranges, promotions, and allocations. These systems were used to decide what the customer wants and to place the product in selected locations based on past performance.

At SAP, we believe that this centralized rear view mirror approach will become less relevant as the full impact of the mobile, social networked consumer puts the customer back in control. This change brings buyers closer to their customer; it allows them to be more focused and provides instant trading and also social media commentary data.

At SAP, we ensure that all the elements covering fashion planning, buying, and supply chain work efficiently together and incorporate customer-centricity at the heart of the processes. This simply means that the right product gets from factory to customer more efficiently, giving the consumer exactly what they want when they want it. The buyer will more and more be able to think globally and act locally, reversing the 'one-size-fits-all' approach of the last 25 years.

Equipping the front-end user interface (the working screens) with more user-friendly interfaces allows people to easily see the important things as they happen in the business.

The notion of "Google fast, Apple friendly" will become intertwined with smartphone technology to drive a new generation of easy-to-use mobile BDSS modules enabling buyers to act quickly, efficiently, and faster than their competitors.

Chapter 4 summary

This chapter has examined in outline the why, how, and who of the planning processes involved with creating a range, in particular, those relative to own-label buying. Getting the right number of lines and ranges to fit varying-sized shops is always a problem, and it is here where the buyer and merchandiser relationship is best explained. The lead-up to the final range, including foreign buying trips and the sampling process has been put into context. The relationship of the buyer to that of other internal functions and external parties, especially the significance of the buyer's relationship with PR and the fashion media, has been explored. This chapter has also looked at the high level of detailed numerical planning, analysis, and control used in modern buying and merchandising practice. Finally, the intense focus on achieving key buying KPIs and ultimately the business's planned profitability has been explained. Remember: despite planning, the buyer's eye and instincts still play a major role in a fashion buyer's critical success!

Questions and discussion points

Now that we have looked at the high importance of planning in fashion buying, consider the following questions, assuming that you are the buyer.

1. If you were buying a jeans range for the current season, what essential styles would a small branch local to you have to stock in order to present a viable range? How many styles would be needed? Make a list.

2. Once you have answered this question, work out how many different sizes, colors, and fabric options would be needed based on the number of styles that you have suggested.

3. Undertake an audit of your own wardrobe and list all the different garments that you own. Once you have done this, analyze this list in terms of the number of garments per category, the number of different fabrics, and the number of different colors. You will be surprised at the total list you compile!

4. Visit your local jeans retailer and make a list of the number of styles that they stock—do you think that the range you came up with is better or worse than theirs?

5. What retail prices would you sell your ideal jeans range at? Do look at the competition to work a set of realistic prices out.

N.B. Feel free to substitute any garment type other than jeans in this exercise.

Exercises

Buyers and merchandisers are expected to be good verbal communicators at the numerous meetings that they attend during the planning process. They also have to be good at recalling detail. Try these exercises to see how hard this can actually be.

1. Select your favorite garment or fashion accessory then quickly describe the garment in detail as though you were talking over the phone to a manufacturer at the other end who could not see it. Try to do this in two minutes.

2. Select your favorite fashion retailer and talk for three minutes explaining why you like them so much. Try to be really specific with the points that you make.

3. Visit the fashion retailer that you love the most along with two key competitors. List any weak or missing aspects of your favorite retailer's current range(s), compared to that of the competition.

4. Visit any fashion retailer; pick one garment type and look hard at the range. Leave the shop and then try to recall as much as you can on paper of what you saw. Go back in and check how accurate your recall actually was.

5. Take any online fashion retailer and analyze how many different styles, colors and sizes they are offering for sale on the web.

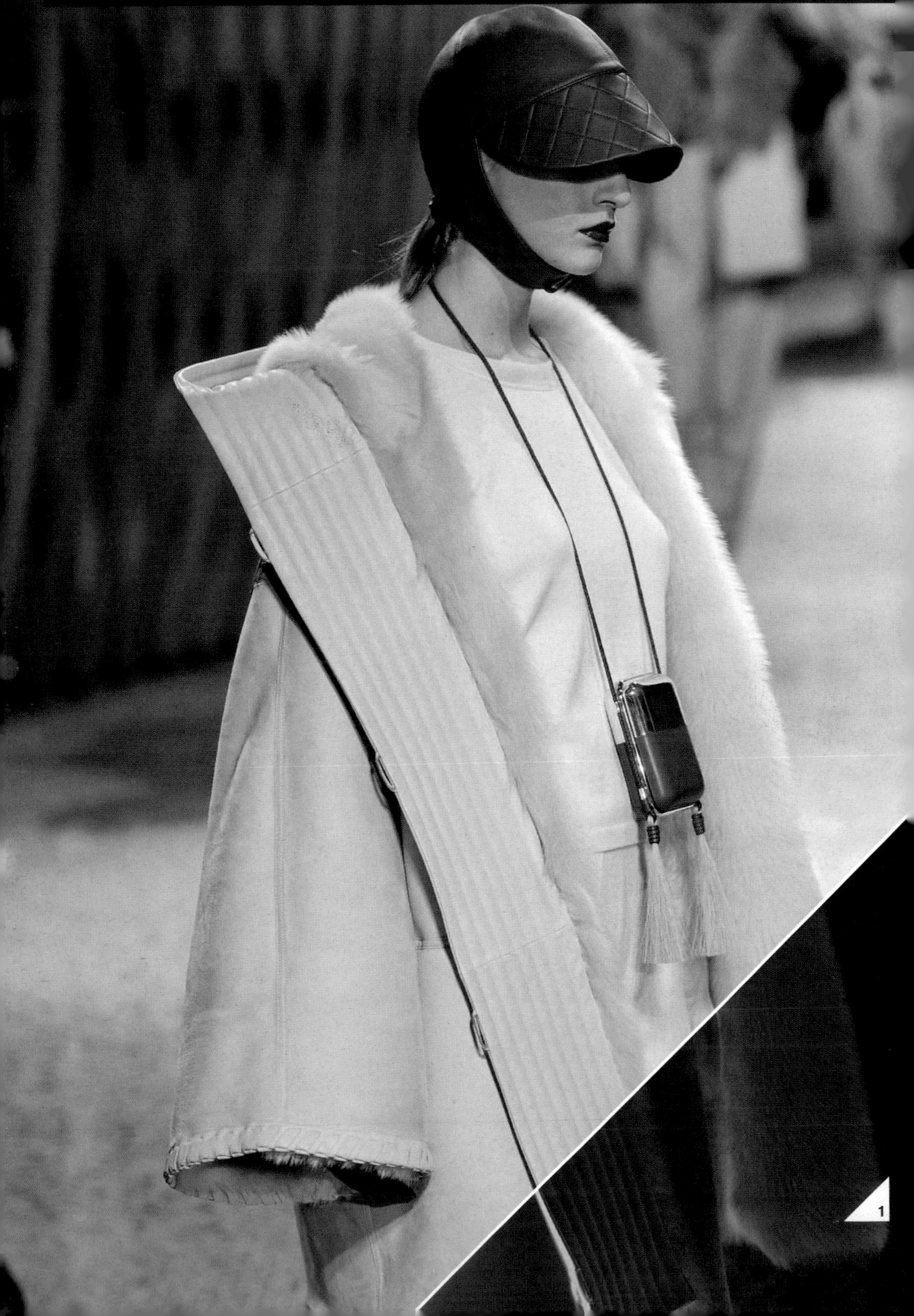

1

5

TRENDS IN FASHION BUYING

In the previous chapters, we have explored the role of the fashion buyer and their working relationships, gaining a basic overview of how the buyer works within retail organizations. We have also looked at trend forecasting and research methodologies, and come to recognize how important it is for buyers to be aware of their consumer demographic and target audiences. An exploration of supplier communication and merchandise planning enabled us to understand how a buyer sources, manufactures, and allocates product alongside merchandisers, thereby ensuring a successful product range on the shop floor. In this final chapter, we will look at emerging trends in the retail industry, and how they can contribute to a buyer's success. These trends include promotional activities, technology, and social responsibility.

1 AUTUMN/WINTER 2011–12

For this season, the luxury leather goods brand Hèrmes developed its first prêt-à-porter collection in order to broaden both its appeal and potential audience.

Promotional activities

Buyers help to set up a number of promotional retail activities, with the aim of achieving a higher gross margin each season while moving units at a more rapid rate. Many of these promotions typically entail some level of discount pricing, but there are also other promotional activities that can help to drive sales without compromising the overall pricing strategy as set by the buying and merchandising teams.

Branding, advertising, and marketing

Often, buyers will work with senior management and marketing teams to create diffusion lines, or subsequent lines of private label goods, which sell for a more moderate price point. Retailers have been doing this for years (think about Old Navy from Gap, for example) and now many designers are beginning to engage in this trend. Fashion designers such as Yohji Yamamoto and Marc Jacobs, have put out diffusion lines (Y's and Marc by Marc Jabobs, respectively) that enable buyers who purchase national brands for lower-priced markets to expand their product range in their retail shops.

Many fast fashion retailers are now offering branded collaborations, which are a way for high-end designers to introduce an affordable line to otherwise nonexistent consumers. These collaborations were already extremely popular with big-box retailers and department stores, but they have now begun to hit fast fashion specialty stores in a big way, too. For instance, H&M has worked with many big names in fashion, such as Karl Lagerfeld, Roberto Cavalli, Marni, and most recently, Versace. The collaborations are typically limited in range and once they sell out, they are not replenished.

While some critics may argue that these collaborations cheapen the high-end designer's image, many feel it is a chance for low-income shoppers to buy into high-end designer goods that they could not otherwise afford. It also introduces a new target audience to an otherwise generic and/or ailing brand making such collaboration a win-win scenario for both parties.

2 RETAILER<>RETAILER COLLABORATIONS

Target has implemented an ongoing partnership program with specialty stores and boutiques, cocreating limited lines of affordable collections to be sold in Target stores. This type of collaboration creates an awareness of small retailers and enables Target to introduce fresh, contemporary brands more frequently to its shelves.

"The celebrity has a built-in network to get word out and raise the profile of the collaboration very quickly, but what collaborations do struggle with is sustainability – how this can not just be 15 minutes of fame."

Mary Ellen Muckerman, Head of Strategy for international consultancy, Wolff Olins

2
3

3 INDUSTRY LEADER CO-BRANDED LINES

Anna Dello Russo, Editor-at-Large and Creative Consultant for *Vogue Japan*, visits a giant bangle built in celebration of her Anna Dello Russo For H&M accessories line during London Fashion Week Spring/Summer 2013 at Covent Garden, London.

Promotional activities

When it comes to advertising and marketing, retailers will pay hefty sums of money to have ads run on billboards, in magazines, or via television, or streaming Internet. While this is a great way for the brand to get exposure, it can put a heavy burden on the buyer who needs to be aware of running (present and future) campaigns that may cause a shift in the popularity of a product.

Advertising and marketing, if successful, will create a need for a product and, if buyers have not purchased enough of that product to be able to provide it to consumers, then consumers may turn elsewhere, sending sales to competing retailers.

While advertising and marketing campaigns will often promote new goods for the season, one of the greatest marketing campaigns is created when a retailer goes into markdown mode, typically adding the clearly marked red-type signage and .99 price points to the shop floor.

While each retailer treats sales promotions differently, the ultimate goal for each is to move through units quickly, making room for new goods to arrive. Buyers work with merchandisers on pricing strategies for both sales and promotions, and then with the marketing teams to create the appropriate signage.

4

4 MOST SOUGHT-AFTER RETAIL PROMOTION

While many consumers resonate with (and are drawn to) various marketing campaigns presented by their favorite retailers, it is the "sale" sign that often prompts consumers to visit retailers; in the hope of finding a bargain.

UNEMPLOYEE OF THE YEAR

ENTRANT:
KATERINA, 30, NON-MANAGER
FROM GREECE.

UNITED COLORS OF BENETTON.

1 OF THE NEARLY
100 MILLION PEOPLE
UNDER 30 YEARS OF AGE
IN SEARCH OF A JOB.

Tell us about your non-work

UNITED COLORS
OF BENETTON.

5

MARKETING AND ADVERTISING INITIATIVES

Retailers use various methods and media to deliver information to consumers. Understanding consumer purchasing behavior (discussed in Chapter 2) allows buyers to work with marketing and/or advertising teams to:

× Increase foot traffic in shop
× Increase units per transaction (UPT), or the amount of goods that a consumer buys per sales transaction
× Introduce new branding initiatives
× Attract new clientele
× Help drive volume during peak seasons or slow periods both in shops or online.

5 GLOBAL MARKETING IMPACTS

An ad campaign for Italian retailer, Benetton, who uses its marketing to not only showcase new product for the season, but also as a forum to raise awareness of the rising levels of youth unemployment. CSR initiatives such as this are discussed later in the chapter.

Promotional activities

Visual merchandising

Earlier in the book, we discussed the ways in which the merchandiser role differs from that of the visual merchandiser. However, it is important to be aware that visual merchandising teams still work very closely with buying/merchandising teams to create aesthetically pleasing visual presentations with the intention of promoting the brand, educating the consumer and, of course, driving sales.

Often, the buyer will work with visual merchandising teams, both at a corporate and store level, to put priorities on certain product that they have bought heavily in. Maintaining constant communication allows visual merchandising teams to understand seasonal investments that are purchased to make the largest profit. It may also be that a buyer wants to test new fits, colors, textiles, and so on, so good communication with visual merchandising teams will allow for quicker feedback on this product.

Buyers need to have open communication lines with the visual merchandising teams so that they are fully aware of the importance of range specifics that will help drive greater sales volume.

100% CASHMERE
SPECIAL OPENING PRICE
$59.90

6 DRIVING SALES THROUGH VISUAL MERCHANDISING

Although buyers do not art direct the visual merchandising approach of a retailer, they will work with visual teams to discuss product placement in specific shop zones, hoping to make deep seasonal buys a focus for all shop members. Communicating seasonal styles, colors, fabrics, and so on will enable the visual merchandising teams to push this product by housing it in focal fixtures, on mannequins or in shop windows.

6

Buyers, along with merchandisers at the senior level, rely on the visual merchandising teams to help drive sales of their product ranges. Without having strong, positive, and consistent relationships with visual merchandising, buyers may find that a visual merchandiser focuses on other attributes of the product range that do not have significant mark-up, creating a slow profit generator for the entire organization. When buyers educate visual merchandising teams on new product or changes in the existing range, the visual merchandising teams can assist in the promotion of this product in a more cohesive manner at shop level.

Visual merchandisers and buyers today form stronger relationships at shop level because it is a good way of buyers gaining valuable insights on replenishment and/or future range purchases. Visual merchandisers for shops will often move up to assistant buyer roles from store level.

Promotional activities

Working with the fashion press

Each season, fashion businesses ensure that they show their ranges to relevant press and media. In the competitive world of fashion, everyone is keen to get as much publicity as possible. Some fashion businesses will undertake their own PR and marketing, while others may outsource these activities.

If approached, fashion buyers will need to become involved with advising on ranges and providing samples to be used at press shows and in publicity packs each season. Fashion journalists from all walks of media are always looking out for new and exciting products and stories for their next fashion features, magazines, and supplements.

Cultivating a strong relationship between the buyer's PR management and the media, together with the production of a strong range for the new season, is likely to mean that a buyer's ranges get strongly featured in the fashion press, potentially generating valuable consumer interest in them.

7 CELEBRITY OUTREACH

Opening ceremonies can be a lucrative investment, drawing attention to both the retail brand and the new shop location. Often, large retailers will hold well-orchestrated events for flagship openings, such as this one for Topshop/Topman in Los Angeles, at which many celebrities attended, including actress Kate Boswell (pictured), who got to view the buyer's seasonal range first hand.

Press packs will often provide key information on store delivery dates and locations—as well as information on sizes, constructions, colors, and pricing. Many fashion companies hire a prestigious venue and have an open house day where new ranges are shown and the fashion media are invited to attend. Press packs (printed folders of photographs, range facts and contact details) and gift bags (often containing product samples) are provided, encouraging the press to attend.

Most fashion companies will utilize a variety of online PR service agencies, which can also provide a wide range of PR-related services, such as online press releases, photographs, archives, and so on. This means that busy journalists, who may not be able to attend a given press day, can quickly and easily get up to speed about a fashion range online. With so many influential fashion bloggers watching the fashion blogosphere, a strong online PR presence is now a vital element of good fashion marketing communication.

Buyers and assistant buyers often attend press days and meet with important fashion media contacts to give them a more personalized tour of the ranges. With so much fashion PR activity taking place today, there is always a huge amount of competition to get important fashion media along to more minor press days or press launches. Buyers with new and exciting ranges, brands, or ideas therefore always attract the more important fashion media.

Providing samples for the press

The fashion press requires new season samples well in advance, in order to develop topical newsworthy stories. Controlling press samples effectively is extremely important, with many being sent away on location and damaged by make-up and general wear and tear.

Good photographic publicity is the lifeblood of successful fashion businesses— those buying teams with the ability to respond quickly and efficiently to the insatiable and sometimes unreasonable demands of the fashion press get the greatest column inches. Having a good relationship with the media and marketing people both within and without the company can pay huge publicity dividends.

The marketing/visual display department also plans window and in-store product displays and promotions well in advance of the season. These are then used to create set window and visual display instructions that are sent out to the local visual merchandising teams.

Maintaining good relationships with all external and internal promotional departments is essential. Having the new season's sample readily available is the greatest help that buying teams can give to support all aspects of marketing activity.

Technology

As the technological age progresses and more consumers conduct personal and business activities from a growing range of devices (PDAs, smartphones, laptops, and so on), transactions have become quicker, more streamlined, and ultimately, more efficient. Buyers are tapping into this technology to overcome communication obstacles and lengthy lead times in pursuit of quicker replenishment turnaround, a stronger consumer understanding and, of course, greater ease in carrying out the duties associated to their job.

Today, technology is delivered in so many formats that it is important for retailers to quickly adapt to changing market trends and specifically, to understand how their consumers conduct business in both brick-and-mortar locations and e-commerce sites. Due to the quickly evolving digital market, buyers are using this technology to react more swiftly to both retail outlets.

"The new information technology...Internet and e-mail...have practically eliminated the physical costs of communications."
Peter Drucker (educator and management consultant)

8

How the Internet has helped buyers

If you can, imagine a time when all business was conducted through landline phone systems, fax machines, and national postal services. These systems, though revolutionary in their time, have now become obsolete in the workplace, having been replaced by digital systems that enable correspondence between parties to take place with minimal effort and expense.

Through the use of various communication protocols, which allow for voice communication and multimedia functions, buyers can get real-time information to conduct their business needs. Internet telephony (voice, facsimile, SMS or short message service) is the preferred method of communication for almost all retail businesses these days.

Buyers can use these systems to carry out various activities and to gather important data, at any given time:

× View, order, and communicate with international manufacturers and suppliers much more efficiently
× Research trends via social media sites, trend forecasting agencies, and/or online periodicals
× Get real-time product sell-through via systems that connect buying offices to shops, allowing them to quickly reorder product
× Capture consumer information to be used in future season's range purchases (i.e. size, color, and silhouette)
× Provide shop teams with imperative information that may impact sales of specific product both positively and negatively.

8 DIGITAL BUSINESS

Buyers can now address production or design issues the very minute that they occur. The speed at which buyers, designers, and merchandisers can now conduct business has revolutionized the fashion industry, making it much more competitive and a smaller place.

Smartphones and QR codes

With the introduction of the smartphone, consumers can easily access their favorite retailers with the touch of an application, linking them directly to the online stores that seem to have an endless array of merchandise. Just as buyers and merchandisers are responsible for ensuring that the right product hits shops at the right time, they must also follow suit to meet e-tailing (electronic retailing) needs too.

Because of the huge growth in e-tailing markets and smartphone usage, buyers can work with marketing teams to create sales promotions and have communication sent directly to the consumer at any given time. The smartphone thus acts as a digital coupon, providing shoppers with discounts, incentives, promotions, and so on.

Many applications for the smartphone have the capability of reading what is known as a quick-response code, or QR code for short. This code, which works similarly to a UPC code, is a matrix barcode which can be converted to URL's, coupons, marketing ads, social media, and so much more. The use of this code has actually become more favourable as a discount module or as a link to URL's to promote retailers' websites. Buyers then have the ability to work with marketing teams to promote seasonal product to a greater audience.

While the smartphone and QR codes are being used more frequently by consumers, retailers are also investing in smartphones for brick-and-mortar plants, using them as mobile POS units to quickly get consumers in and out of the register lines, rather than queueing to make their purchases.

As soon as the purchase or return has been made by the consumer, buyers can receive immediate digital correspondence regarding the items sold or returned, making the reordering of merchandise much more streamlined. With traditional cashiering methods, buyers would have had to wait for the weekly sales reports to be generated, whereas now, they can begin the replenishment process much faster, as the information filters in.

9 TECHNOLOGY DRIVES SALES

Retailers use the Internet, smartphones and QR codes to promote, advertise, and market their brand and goods. Buying teams use it to track sales within stores for quicker replenishment as well as for gauging which items from the seasonal buying range are most profitable and which are the most slow-selling. Technology is also a way for buying and merchandising teams to further understand their consumer demographics.

9

Corporate social responsibility

Buying teams have a responsibility to themselves, to the company that they work for and, most importantly, to the consumer purchasing goods sold in retail outlets. Often called CSR for short, corporate social responsibility is the self-imposed regulatory system that a retailer builds into their business plan and company mission. The objective is to seamlessly integrate people, planet, and profit into a module that can work to create sustainable measures for all three elements.

While the term CSR is fairly young, stemming from corporations in the late 20th century who were looking to protect shareholders, the concept of ethical decision making for the greater good has long been a practice carried out by many small business owners and non-profit organizations.

In retail, ethical decision making comes in many forms, from abiding by international trade laws to fair/equal wages paid to all employees. When a retailer decides to grow its business with CSR initiatives, it typically maps out an overall plan for long-term growth and will then start with small tasks that won't drastically deplete revenue, allowing it to grow in a positive direction.

Each employee, knowing that the company has identified specific initiatives, will then be required to help achieve these goals, both in the short and long term. In addition to the company initiatives, each employee bears the responsibility of monitoring their own ethical behavior, in an effort to help the retailer to reach their intended goal.

CSR STAKEHOLDERS

Many individuals, companies, and communities are part of CSR outreaches:

× Employees—those working in the field and at corporate offices, from senior management to maintenance
× Customers—past, present, and future customers who buy into the company brand
× Communities—the areas and individuals who are part of the physical environment where shops or home offices are located
× Suppliers—both national and international, as well as the employees of the suppliers
× Investors—those who want to see the company grow but typically only provide monetary means or consulting services.

"Consumers have not been told effectively enough that they have huge power and that purchasing and shopping involve a moral choice."

Anita Roddick (founder of The Body Shop)

WORKPLACE

people + planet + profit =

CORPORATE SOCIAL
RESPONSIBILITY

COMMUNITY

ENVIRONMENT

MARKETPLACE

10 CSR CYCLE

Corporate social responsibility
initiatives involve multiple
entities within the context of
social, environmental, and
economic values. It is important
to understand how each is
dependent on the other and how
lack of initiative for one could
seriously affect the others, both
positively and negatively.

10

Corporate social responsibility

Each stakeholder within the retail organization has a responsibility to uphold the CSR initiatives set out by the owners, operators, or senior management of the company. Each employee within the organization also has their own set of personal values and judgments that they personally adhere to, which may sometimes encroach on the company's, in either a good or a bad way.

Buyers deal with many suppliers on a daily basis and should be aware of their CSR initiatives, just as they are of their own. When a buyer forms new relationships, they should investigate how the supplier conducts business, and how it treats both its employees and the environment.

Many overseas vendors do not pay fair wages, and may not provide adequate facilities, or breaks for their employees. If a buyer does not immediately recognize this situation, it does not however mean that they should ignore situations that may later cause tension between stakeholders and the firm. Enquiring right at the start of a new relationship about a company's practices— and continually following up these enquiries to ensure that circumstances have not changed—will ensure that the buyer is working towards their company's CSR initiatives, or at the very least good moral judgment.

11–12 ONE FOR ONE

A quickly emerging leader in the CSR movement is shoe retailer, TOMS, whose founder, Blake Kycoskie, made it his goal to provide one pair of shoes to a child in need for every pair that he sold. This CSR initiative was so successful that TOMS recently began a secondary initiative with sunglasses: for each pair sold, TOMS donates one pair of prescription glasses.

12

In the event that a buyer should learn of such situations, it is best to report or log this information, before informing senior management. Sometimes, if the company is large enough and the supplier risks losing valuable business (and earning a poor reputation), it may invest in ways to rectify the situation, thus turning things round for both parties.

Another situation that occurs frequently in buying offices is the presentation of gifts by suppliers, sometimes out of courtesy but more often as a means to keep future business. As discussed in Chapter 3, the relationship between buyer and supplier should remain very professional at all times. Accepting gifts, trips, or personal discounts is typically against most company policies, as is forming personal relationships with suppliers outside the office.

Buyers should also look to purchase product that is more environmentally friendly, both in pre- and post-production. The textile industry is one of the heaviest polluters in the industry, so sourcing vendors that take strides to reclaim dye water or use recycled fibers can be an easy way to satisfy a quickly growing sustainable consumer base. Be aware that suppliers in foreign countries may avoid discussing sustainable practices, especially if they don't engage in any.

A buyer who continually asks questions of their suppliers regarding these topics can help to change business practices that were previously unethical, or just not well thought-through. Consumers are more aware of their retailer's practices and will gladly choose one over another if their purchasing practices are negatively affecting communities or the environment. A good buyer will adhere to their company's CSR practices, as well as their own personal judgment should those practices unwittingly go awry.

Corporate social responsibility

Most buyers are concerned about design originality and the authenticity of the lines that they propose to buy. A question often posed to designers and manufacturers is: "Is this design truly original?". Fashion, due to its fast-changing nature, is a minefield with many designers and brands frequently being copied by other individuals or organizations, who then offer a cheaper version of an original designer or branded product to a wider market.

The intellectual property right (IPR) attached to the copied product, whoever owns it, is effectively stolen to make profit for another organization and/or individual. In many cultures, copying is not seen as a crime, although increasingly individuals and organizations are developing techniques, laws, and/or systems to protect their IP from the unscrupulous. Anti Copying in Design (ACID), a useful organization with good advisory resources that was founded in 1996 is now helping fashion businesses and designers to avoid IP issues (www.acid.uk.com).

Unique fashion and textile surface designs can be registered in the UK, Europe, and many other non-EU countries. However, the registration processes and costs vary dramatically and for many smaller companies and designers, doing so is simply not financially viable.

ETHICAL DECISION MAKING

Many fast fashion retailers will quickly produce similar fashions to those of luxury and exclusive boutique designers. This poses an ethical problem for consumers, as they observe their favorite inexpensive retailers continually battling in the courtrooms with those designers whose work they have allegedly copied.

In 2011, there was a highly public lawsuit between fast fashion retailer, Forever 21 and womenswear start up, Feral Childe. The lawsuit was situated around a textile pattern that was used on a series of garments produced by Forever 21 that Feral Childe claimed to have originally designed.

This was a highly publicized case that had many consumers concerned about the social responsibility of fast fashion retailers. Because little was known about the design process operated by Forever 21, it also made it difficult for those who want to support retailers with strong CSR initiatives to do so with the company.

Other retailers have addressed the same issue of infringement of copyright with Forever 21 regarding their own designs, but all cases have been settled out of court.

13 CANAL STREET SHOPS

In New York, tourists flock to Canal Street in lower Manhattan in search of low-priced designer goods that you are unlikely to find in major retailers. Here, shop owners often have "silent salesmen" who invite street patrons to back rooms where designer knock-offs and stolen goods are sold at deeply discounted prices.

13

Design registration is an immensely complex process, but fashion buyers and readers can find many online advisory resources. One of the best sources of UK and European IP advice is to be found at the Centre for Fashion Enterprise, based in London (www.fashion-enterprise.com). On a more international basis, The World Intellectual Property Organization, based in Geneva, is also a good source for pan-international IP advice relating to fashion (www.wipo.int).

When fashion buyers raise official business contracts, these generally include caveats warning suppliers about the need for authenticity and uniqueness in their products and designs; this helps to protect the buyer and their organization from any future legal challenges. In reality, all fashion garments and products probably take inspiration from each other: after all, is anything totally unique?

Buyers need to remain aware of these situations and strive to keep the market clean of stolen designs and inauthentic merchandise. While this may be part of the organization's overall CSR direction, buyers will typically follow their own instincts on this front, knowing how detrimental it can be for the company to engage in unethical practices; and more importantly, in order to maintain their own clear conscience.

Case study: Hennes & Mauritz (H&M)

Hennes & Mauritz (H&M) is one of the world's most successful international fashion retailers today. This Swedish-based organization, founded in 1947 by Erling Persson, now operates over 2,600 stores in 47 markets and is the second largest clothing retailer in the world. Not only is H&M a successful fast fashion retailer; the company also maintains strong CSR initiatives, paving ways for other retailers to follow suit.

H&M offers fashion and quality at affordable prices for men, women, teenagers, and children, using a team of over 140 in-house designers, as well as a large internal team of buyers and pattern makers based in Sweden. H&M is a very people-orientated business and there is a great team spirit running through the whole organization.

The company promotes an employee-centric business, believing in continuous improvement for and team cooperation among its staff body, while at the same time being very profit-driven and cost-conscious. Open-mindedness is encouraged in staff across all areas of the company.

Unlike many fashion operations, H&M does not directly own or control its factories, preferring instead to work with over 700 independent suppliers, located mainly throughout Asia and Europe. In over 20 manufacturing countries, H&M has local production offices, staffed mainly by nationals, who liaise with and advise local manufacturers directly.

The local production offices also take control of and manage safety and quality testing, as well as ensuring that all products are made at the right price. H&M is a master of fast fashion and has developed the ability to target its products to suit the nuances of each different market that it enters.

H&M creates simple modern designs with a global and universal appeal. Generally, H&M prefers to directly own and operate its international store chain; although in a few markets, it sometimes works with a franchise partner.

In common with many Scandinavian-based organizations, H&M is a strong supporter of sustainability and to that end supports many green initiatives in the countries where it trades. It also likes to ensure that workers in the factories that it uses are well treated. Following an incident in its Cambodian factory in 2012, H&M has worked closely with the International Labour Organization (ILO), to ensure that its Cambodian factory workers enjoy good working conditions and terms of employment.

H&M is increasingly becoming more involved with the factory conditions of its chosen manufacturing sources. Other social initiatives that H&M has undertaken include extensive charitable work. For example, the company has raised around $4.5m through a five-year partnership program with UNICEF, and has launched a textile recycling program in their brick-and-mortar locations.

14 STRONG SALES TO MATCH A STRONG CSR INITIATIVE

H&M is always making headlines, especially when it comes to business practices. They continually open new flagships across the globe and keep pushing the envelope in store design and visual merchandising, as seen here in this exterior view of the Ginza, Japan store and interior view in Düsseldorf, Germany.

Case study: Hennes & Mauritz (H&M)

One of the unique marketing approaches taken by H&M has been a series of regular collaborations with leading international fashion designers, celebrities, and fashion bloggers. Twice a year, a guest designer will produce a limited edition for sale within H&M. Small collections have been sold in selected large H&M stores, although the scope and scale of each collection is generally a closely guarded secret.

Although judged by the trade to be a relatively small part of their total annual turnover, the publicity generated by these designer launches is massive and helps to keep H&M at the leading edge of fashion. The early morning queues and in-store rush for these products has even resulted in acts of violence between customers, desperate to get a piece of the action and purchase garments by designers that they wouldn't otherwise be able to afford!

Key designers to have been involved with the multinational brand so far include Karl Lagerfeld, Stella McCartney, Viktor & Rolf, Madonna, Roberto Cavalli, Kylie Minogue, Comme des Garçons, Matthew Williamson, Jimmy Choo, Sonia Rykiel, Elin Ling, Versace, Lanvin, Marni, and Maison Martin Margiela—with many more famous names rumored to be lined up for future launches.

In every country, the buying team of H&M are incredibly successful in delivering the right level of fashion to their customers. H&M is the world's leading and most well-focused international fashion retail buying operation, with an unrivaled universal appeal to the young people of the world. The simplicity of their operation and their clear and demonstrable understanding of today's global consumer are second to none. H&M's buying operation is its greatest strength which, combined with the clear vision of its directors, continues year after year, enabling the business to continue to expand and trade successfully.

The H&M group has acquired and is developing other branded fashion operations to add to its operations— including COS, Monki, Weekday, and Monday. Each of these brands is differently positioned and targeted to the main H&M brand offer and may provide a springboard for further international expansion. H&M home goods stores have also opened to target the home accessories market. Savvy business leadership and strong CSR initiatives, coupled with an unbeatable buying/merchandising team, put H&M far above its competitors.

H&M is a master of fast fashion and has developed the ability to target its products to suit the nuances of each different market that it enters.

15 H&M CONSCIOUS COLLECTION

Actress Emmy Rossum attends Global Green USA's 10th Anniversary Pre-Oscar Party sponsored by H&M in Hollywood, California.

15

Chapter 5 summary

In this chapter, we explored trends in fashion buying and looked at how customer-centric buying is a key element of all successful fashion buying. The fast-changing nature of consumer fashion in relation to the rapid and significant rise of fast fashion was discussed, a concept now central to most young fashion buying operations.

We looked at the role of the buyer in relation to promotional activities geared towards discount pricing, pricing strategies (in conjunction with merchandisers), the creation of diffusion lines, and branded collaborations to explore how buyers can be instrumental in enabling low-income shoppers to buy into high-end designer goods—a key driver of sales. Successful advertising and marketing initiatives rely on a solid understanding of consumer purchasing behavior; as much as they do on strong communication with visual merchandising colleagues and the building of effective relationships with the press.

Keeping up to speed with the latest technological advances, such as the use of QR codes, enables buyers to stay ahead of their competitors. Likewise, buyers need to keep abreast of both industry and consumer trends, such as sustainability, in order to keep on top of their game.

In the following exercise, we will now explore the importance of the fashion focus group to the buying process.

Questions and discussion points

Working in groups of between five to seven people, imagine that you are about to launch a young, innovative fashion shoe retail chain in your own town, aimed at consumers between the ages of 15–24. One person should assume the role of focus group facilitator and the exercise will involve you all in planning and carrying out a focus group exercise.

The buyers are unclear about a few issues relating to key areas of buying interest and want them clarified before setting about developing and buying the range. The role of your focus group is to help them understand what to do by running a discussion using the questions below as starting points; this should run for a maximum of 30–40 minutes.

1. What should the balance be between casual and formal shoes in the shop?

2. What does the focus group understand by the terms "formal" and "casual"—can they specify what they associate them with?

3. Are there any "must-have" branded shoes that should be included in the opening range?

4. What types of brands of shoes are not readily available in competing stores in your area/town?

5. Are there any other issues that the focus group feel or believe that the buyer should be aware of relating to the possible range to be developed?

Exercise

1. Create a seating plan so that the group can sit around and discuss the issues outlined in this exercise.

2. One person should be designated to take notes and ideally record the conversation on a mobile phone, for analysis and clarification later.

3. The focus group facilitator should use the list of questions to get everyone to contribute. It will quickly become clear that some people may have extreme, unworkable, or irrelevant views—but do listen to everyone.

4. The facilitator must take control and keep everyone focused on the topic at hand. People often tend to stray away from a subject as they talk, so it's important to bring the subject back into the discussion when this happens.

5. At the end of the discussion, everyone should review the notes that have been made and together write a brief bullet-pointed note advising the buyer of the group's main findings. Many points made will be irrelevant or inconsequential. It is amazing what you can find out by talking to a group of targeted customers!

CONCLUSION

Fashion buying is an important role defined by an expansive and ever-evolving industry. Each retailer hires, trains, mentors, and develops the individuals within their teams, hoping to in turn receive consumer recognition that their product lines are fashion-forward must-haves that simultaneously have the capacity to generate profits for the organization.

The buyer's role, as discussed throughout this book, is a rigorous one, often compounded by extensive meetings, long travel hours, and strenuous deadlines, which keep the buyer continually moving. Time management is of the upmost importance, as a buyer has to juggle many hats at once. Building strong relationships with coworkers within the organization can help to alleviate some of the stress that naturally comes with the job.

A buyer's strongest partnership will always be with the merchandiser, the individual who helps to facilitate the planning of merchandise from inception to store deliveries. These two individuals will together create buying and allocation strategies that will enable their shops to maximize their sales through speedy shipment deliveries and re-stocking, but more importantly—that will create brand differentiation for the retailer.

When buyers source out existing and/or new suppliers and manufacturers, they cultivate external relationships that will also help to strengthen their position. Thanks to various technological advances in communication and logistics, buyers have the capability to speak directly to globally sourced agencies, preventing risk and range issues from occurring prior to development of the line. Having professional relationships that act in the best interests of the buyer's employer is the only way that a buyer will remain as a respected (and employed!) team player for as long as they remain within the industry.

In the latter part of the book, we explored emerging trends in the retail sector and how they influence the buyer, both positively and negatively. These trends, which may eventually become industry norms, are ways for the buyer to further understand their consumer market while working to gain new customers for what is hopefully an already successful retailer.

Being aware of the various stakeholders under their retail organization's umbrella will allow the buyers to think consciously about the decisions they make and how they will likely impact their firm, consumers, suppliers and ultimately, themselves.

The concept of corporate social responsibility is becoming vital practice in a quickly expanding global economy. Understanding their organization's initiatives, as well as the initiatives of their stakeholders, will keep the fashion buyer educated as they work towards their profit goals, as their seasonal ranges mature from trend forecast to shop floor.

We hope that you have enjoyed reading this book and that it helps you on your way to a successful career in fashion buying!

APPENDIX

1 SPRING/SUMMER
2010

Philip Lim's prêt-à-porter
womenswear combines
1930s elegance with
statuesque heels, adding a
contemporary flourish to this
celebrated silhouette.

1

Glossary

Few buyers are fully cognizant of all the legal and quasi-legal aspects mentioned here, but all should have a working knowledge of each to enable them to identify when professional legal advice is needed. In general, copying and design infringement is becoming more of a hot topic to fashion buying, as brands and designers—in common with society in general—are becoming more litigious. Buyers must do everything in their power to confirm that a design they select is not a direct or covert copy—sometimes also called a "knock off."

Brand names
A registered name, term, design, symbol, or other feature that easily identifies one seller's product or service from any other.

Brick-and-mortar locations
The physical plant at which a retailer or wholesaler will sell their goods or services to consumers.

Consumer demographics
Those elements that define the organization's customer profile and are defined by ethnicity, income, age, and education. Consumer demographics are quantifiable data which is used typically for marketing purposes.

Corporate social responsibility
A voluntary code created by individual corporations relating to the organization's ethical and environmental stance in its dealings with all of its stakeholders.

Counterfeiting
The deliberate copying of branded merchandise in order to pass it off as the genuine article.

Design
The unique look of a fashion product, in which design, aesthetics, or natural beauty have been applied to clothing or accessories, differentiating them from any other.

E-commerce
Refers to an industry that sells goods or services via electronic delivery methods such as the Internet or other various electronic networks.

E-tailing
The term used to denote a retailer who sells goods or services through electronic methods, specifically the Internet. However this term is loosely used to denote any selling method that is not brick and mortar.

Key performance indicators (KPIs)
Different criteria set forth by an organization as a means for measuring performance. KPIs may be based on sales data, consumer market information, etc. to set a standard level of performance practice.

Licensing
The legalized agreement for another party to manufacture or trade a fashion brand, trademark, design, or patent without fear of legal action.

Merchandising
A term used to represent the promotion of goods sold by retailers and/or the allocation of goods to retailers based on various indicators such as consumer need or fashion trends. One who acts to provide these services on behalf of the retailer is called a merchandiser.

National and international product standards

Certain garments and accessories, especially those relating to young children, have to meet stringent national and/or international safety standards, for example in relation to the flammability of children's nightwear.

National brands

Those goods which are produced and distributed by the manufacturer to various retailers; who buy the goods wholesale, redistributing them to their consumers. National brands can be distributed both to national and international markets.

Patents

A legally registered novel or non-obvious product, process, or treatment that has intellectual property protection in a/several jurisdiction/s.

Private label

Brands that are produced and distributed by a manufacturer, through the manufacturer's own retail outlets. These brands are typically not offered to other retailers.

Qualitative research

A type of research that is collected through the observation of human behavior and sensory feedback. It is often gathered through the practice of participant observations, non participant observations, case studies, and ethnographs.

Quantitative research

A type of research that looks at various mathematical models and statistical data which is analyzed to determine a hypothesis or theory.

Return to vendor (RTV)

A term used in the buying office to denote those goods that have been selected to return to the vendor due to poor quality, slow sales, or any other issues deemed necessary for this action.

Stakeholders

Those individuals that will be directly affected by the firms actions or can directly affect the firm or organization, in a positive or negative manner.

Stock-keeping unit (SKU)

A term used to denote the method by which a retailer provides inventory management for their goods and services. Each item for sale is provided with a unique SKU that provides information such as division, class, origin, season, price, materiality, size, color, and so on for the retailer to track for inventory purposes.

Supply chain

The set of firms that make and distribute goods and/or services to consumers. This includes manufacturers, suppliers, wholesalers, retailers, and the consumer.

Trademarks

A distinctive, unique, and usually legally registered sign or indicator that helps consumers to realize which organization a fashion product or service emanates from.

Trade secrets

Any competitively sensitive information/a unique way of conducting business that is not openly understood or able to be viewed.

Visual merchandising

A term used to represent the promotion of goods sold by retailers through the use of display techniques which includes product placement, fixturing, and environmental design (by means of visual design, art, and craft). One who acts to provide these services is called a visual merchandiser.

Industry resources

Fashion buyers, like all of us, tend to trawl their favorite fashion sites as a leisure activity. However, in a business context, they would tend to use business information services. The better services are subscription-based, although there are also many consumer-focused fashion and styling sites. Whether business or consumer focused, many have differing focuses and information offers—often, they are difficult to easily categorize.

Trend forecasting agencies

Fashion buyers rely a great deal upon their designers and trend forecasting services to help make sense of the deluge of dates, information, and facts available to them. Never in the history of fashion have we been faced with so much information. This is one trend that seems likely to continue.

Doneger Group
A New York based trend forecasting agency.

doneger.com

Pantone
International color authority providing a standard in color language from design to manufacturing. Pantone also provides seasonal color forecasts to most industries.

pantone.com

Promostyl
This France-based agency produce a series of Trendbooks, which are designed to anticipate the current trends in design, fashion, and marketing in order to give their clients a strategic edge in the marketplace. They also provide consulting services on all phases of brand, collection, and product design.

promostyl.com

Stylesight
Another important paid trend and information source, which is also UK-based.

stylesight.com/en/home

Trendland
A website which contains exciting trend information on both fashion and design.

trendland.com

Worth Global Style Network (WGSN)
UK-based trend service delivering what is probably the widest available range of online fashion-business-related services.

wgsn.com

Public and subscription services

There are many free fashion blogs and information sites available online. Some of the sites worth checking out are listed below:

Apparel search
A US-based site about trend forecasting services.

apparelsearch.com/index.htm

Awwwards
Internet design creativity in fashion.

awwwards.com/50-fashion-websites.html

Drapers
Site of UK trade-focused *Drapers* fashion magazine.

info.drapersonline.com

Fashionista
An online fashion news blog.

fashionista.com

FJobs
An international site promoting a plethora of fashion jobs around the world as well as industry-breaking news and information.

fashionjobs.com

Style Careers
One of the most respected websites for posting international fashion jobs.

stylecareers.com

Talisman Fashion
An international recruiting agency that focuses on the fashion industry.

talismanfashion.com

uk.fashionmag.com
A UK-centric fashion news site.

uk.fashionmag.com/news/list/Retail,15.html

Visual Merchandising/Store Design (VMSD)
A site geared more toward store design and visual merchandising, VMSD also provides industry updates, introduces new technology, and presents various merchandising strategies.

vmsd.com

Women's Wear Daily (WWD)
Site of the US trade-focused Women's Wear Daily fashion magazine.

wwd.com/

Index

Index

Acknowledgments and picture credits

With special thanks:

From David
I would like to thank the following for their help with the writing of this book, together with thanks to all my fellow fashion academics, students, and friends at The Dublin Institute of Technology, the London College of Fashion and London Metropolitan University: Simon Clark; Lucy Hailey; Judy Head; Stephen Henley; Janet Holbrook; Matthew Jeatt; Bob Jolley; Louise Koser; June Lawlor; Dids Macdonald; and Liam O'Farrell. I would also like to thank my editor Colette Meacher for encouraging me and helping me—and who was wonderfully dedicated and supportive, as part of the team at Bloomsbury. Thanks also to Nigel and Dimitri for their involvement in the project.

From Dimitri
Many thanks go out to Amanda Lovell, AiNYC Fashion Chair for taking a chance on me as a new instructor, thus allowing me to meet so many amazing individuals who have helped to bring this book to fruition – Georgia Kennedy, David Shaw, and ESPECIALLY Colette Meacher, and Nigel Truswell, who worked so patiently with me in the very short amount of time that I was involved with this project. A very special thank you to the Raglands and the Koumbis's, who have been nothing but amazing to me, throughout school and my career. Tate—happy 10 years together, I could not have done any of this without you by my side!

Picture credits:

Getty Images: cover image, 12–13, 14, 19, 20 (2), 22, 24, 25, 29 (left), 33 (3), 34, 35 (2), 46, 48 (left), 50–51 (2), 54, 55, 56 (2), 61, 63, 76 (right), 78–79, 80, 95 (2), 110–111 (3), 112, 114, 118–119, 128–129, 141 (2), 142–143, 143, 144–145, 146–147, 148–149, 150–151, 154–155, 157, 158, 161

Go Runway: 6, 10, 44, 74, 88, 96, 97, 106, 122, 126–127, 138, 167

Kristen Lucio: 3 (photographer: Gabe Tapia, copyright KroweNYC.com, 2013), 36 (copyright KroweNYC.com, 2013), 398 (photographer: Kristen Lucio, copyright BadlandsVintage.com, 2013), 39 (top – photographer: Gabe Tapia, copyright KroweNYC.com, 2013; bottom – copyright KroweNYC.com, 2013)

Promostyl: 66–69

PR Shots: 48, 98–99, 158, 161

PYMCA: 28 (2), 29 (right)

Rex Features: 15, 90–91 (bottom left)

Shutterstock: 58, 59 (2), 60 (2), 62 (top), 76 (left), 77, 81, 86–7 (top left and right; bottom right), 92

Topshop: 124–125

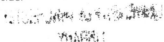